CW01664423

Poems from the Heron Clan III

Edward Lyons and Doug Stuber, editors

Katherine James Books
Chapel Hill

Poems from the Heron Clan III

Katherine James Books

Please find acknowledgements at the back of the book.

ISBN: **978-0-9673855-5-6**

0 9 8 7 6 5 4 3 (who invented this?)

Table of Contents

Phil Morse	1
Pam Bagget	7
Stan Absher	11
Asha Gowan	15
Vivekanand Jha	23
Deborah Hall	28
Robert Okaji	30
Dianne DeCaire	34
Angelaurelio Soldi	36
Yeon-SeongPark	40
Arnold Johanson	44
Ruth Carlin	50
Bruce Lader	54
Priscilla McCelvey	58
Grady Bennett Myers, Jr.	64
Jenna Leigh Evans	68
Doug Stuber	70
Jaki Shelton Green	74
Frank Doonan	85
Renata Lader	90
Edward Lyons	93
Holly Holt	105
Joseph Milford	109
Jasmine Farrrell	113
Preston Martin	118
Kitty Bergel	120
Ramon Ramirez	125
Amanda Gordon	127
Paul Aaron	129
Murry Handler	133
Meg Wethington	136
Richard Smyth	140
Steve Bloom	149
Biographies	152
Acknowledgements	156
Art Biographies	158

Phil Morse

Life Cry

I lie beside you
Listening in the black hour
To your quiet breathing

As the lake laps
In soothing rhythm
Against dark shores.

The aspens in the full night
Rustle with a stirring breeze
As rain drops fall in gentle cadence.

The full moon
Shines brightly through our window
With shadows no sun can cast.

And then a loon call
His sound lonely to us, not him---
The cry of life so clear, so unknowable.

Remembering Peter

For all who stay,
Life can be beauty.
Its loveliness lingers,
Full of sweet dreams
Passing not into nothingness but
To the full glory
Of those who remember you
And hope
Beyond the tender of the night.

Memories

Do you remember the time when you awoke
to find the night's snowfall
closing your school and you had all day
to make snow tunnels and forts?

Can you recall the days spent
with your grandparents who told you stories
and gave you jobs you loved to do
because you were helping them?

Are you able to pull up the aches and joys
of long bike rides to school, your collie dog,
the first time you kissed a girl
who wore too much lipstick?

Do you wish you could go back to that life
of uncluttered simplicity
where you dreamed and played
and didn't have to taste life as it really is?

She Walks in Alone

Too late for the bus,
I drove her to school today.
She walks in alone,
A five year old
Carrying her bookbag,
Her shoulders slouching slightly.
Mostly she leaves on the run,
Still a solitary figure
Making her way in an uncertain world
Her blond hair blowing behind her.

The Awakening

If you asked me how it happened
I'd have to laugh and plead ignorance.
I suddenly saw for the first time ever
A raindrop on a Maple leaf.

The Leaf

If you asked how it happened
as I sat under the maple tree
I'd have to laugh
as a single leaf
bright red and fluttering
fell on my hand
a perfect heart
except for a tear
clean as a paper cut
edge to edge.
And suddenly I saw
not a flawed piece of nature
but life itself, my life
echoing the naked awareness
of who I really am
in the oneness of it all.

A Soprano Voice on Silver Lake, New Hampshire

When I was a teenager
and alone in the still night
of a White Mountain summer
listening to the loons and frogs
with a full moon over the lake below me,
I heard the swish of a canoe paddle
and then the sounds
of a clear soprano voice singing
softly to herself
a dark figure sitting in a canoe
moving slowly past our dock
with the notes becoming fainter
as she glided around the cove.
Fifty years later her voice echoes
as sweet and pure as the night she sang
when life stood still and for once made sense.

The Operation

Hour after hour he sat by his wife's bedside
While tubes dripped and the heart monitor clicked.
The doctor had just explained the risk

In cold, clinical terms:
"You have a greater than usual chance of mortality
Because the hole in your heart lies in a difficult place."

They talked about her increasing exhaustion,
Their two year old who wondered where mommy was.
And then each nurse on the floor took their turn
And hugged her for the time had come.
He watched her being wheeled away---
She waved wanly, blew a kiss, managed a weak smile,
And was gone.

Silence

The snowflakes are many and large
As they fall on the black, cold street in front of me.
I drive alone through a deserted night
On my way to mail a last minute Christmas card
Taking extra side streets
Because I never want this moment to end.

My Son Wishing Me Goodbye

When I left that winter afternoon
with a light snow falling
to begin my new far-away job,
you stood there in the basement
with your four-year-old sniffly nose
saying goodbye
and wanting a farewell kiss one more time.

You had drawn a happy rabbit,
posted on the cellar door,
to cheer me up when I came back.
I would be gone for weeks---all the time
thinking about our trips to the park playground,
our naptime stories, and your questions
about life. And your eyes, asking
why I wouldn't play with you
when other duties called.

I remember your soft "I'll miss you,"
waving goodbye from a second story window

between the snowflakes
as I pulled out of the driveway, a moment
forever frozen because, years later,
from that very day, you walked
into a garage
and hanged yourself.

Mailing a Card on Christmas Eve

Falling on the dark street in front of me,
snowflakes glisten from the shine of street lamps.
On this strange earth I drive alone
to mail a last minute card
thinking about next morning's joy
but also the ugliness of everyman.

It doesn't make sense---
the madness of mind-based self
always thinking, never still
needing to label, conceptualize, judge.

And then a single snowflake lands on my arm
as I open the mailbox.
Words and thoughts disappear
as I lock into its tiny beauty
of Atman consciousness.

Hearing a Phoebe Sing

If you are hurting, so am I
And, as we do, the sun rises
And moves with perfect precision
As waves break on beaches
Over pebbles that know no grief.

And in the distance
Listen to the Phoebe
As it sings the unceasing beauty
Of life beyond sorrow and joy
And of things we are barely aware.

What Really Matters

The sweetest soul love
cannot be parted nor swept aside
by pain body ego or fear
but rather takes wing and alights
in the memory of gardens bathed in white,
of seashores and precious walks
with the melodies of happy people.

The song they sing
is one of beauty and joy
known but to all
as its loveliness lingers
full of sweet dreams
passing into the infinite tenderness
of that which can never be lost.

On the Beach

I'm alone again on the beach.
The softly whistling wind through spruce trees
Cushions happy, robust echoing of distant, childish voices
As a circling fly lands and buzzes away.

.The gray-blue stillness of barely rippling water
Echoes the calm within.
A hummingbird hovers beside a scarlet flower trumpet
Balancing life's hopes, life's struggles on perfectly beating wings.

Thoughts by a Lake

The gentle sand merging with lapping waves
Opens silent thoughts and inner realms
Where my heart, listening, beats strongly
While the wind tosses ferns nearby.

Thought patterns ease as the
Timelessness of past and present whispers
The voice of eternity and I begin
To lose myself in the lake-depths
Of all that is you.

Pam Bagett

Joy

If I could I would go right now to the greenhouse
and pot up some tender seedlings, just to feel the pleasure
of dirt gritty beneath my fingertips. But it's dark out.
Tree frogs are piping music from oak to hickory,
and joy is rising in me as I spoon ice cream
from the open carton. Joy was with me earlier, too,
when I stepped outside to smell the sweet mimosa
and earlier still when I broke bits of leftover hamburger
into my dying dog's dish. Joy in the photo of a pale
mauve clematis pinned to my wall, in bare feet
and the cool dampness of a humid July night.
Joy in this rare coolness so unlike the hellish steambath
I could be stewing in tomorrow. In open windows
and moths that slip through holes in screens
to suicide against the incandescent joy of light bulbs.
Joy abundant as the cracks in farmhouse walls
and ants across the counters, even joy—almost—
in mice that steal across them, but no, that would be asking
too much. But joy, yes, in mice outdoors, and yes,
in tree frogs singing and yes stars shining
and yes the sweet mimosa, yes.

Pompeii Fairy Tale

Let's say he remembered him, this man
who left his dog chained to the wall
as Vesuvius barked and howled
and people ran rabid through the streets.
Let's say he adored his simple mutt
as if it were his child, let's say
he wasn't buried in ash and fire a mile away,
oblivious to the froth at the dog's mouth
as it gnawed the implacable chain.
Let's say the man turned and pushed
against the fleeing crowd fierce
in its animal panic, let's say he got close
enough to call out comfort to his wailing friend.
Let's say he died trying to save him.

Rehrersburg, Pennsylvania, 1857

She slips out past the steaming kettle,
her mother turning bacon that sizzles
in the pan. Snatches an extra jacket
from the porch's hook, the woolen lining
iced with cold. Yesterday's rake leans
on a pile of leaves that Amanda races past,
anxious to escape her family's view.
She works the gate latch until it opens,
snags her sleeve and hears it rip
but she runs on, hefty in her layers,
which are getting too warm. In the orchard,
the last shriveled apples. Amanda stuffs
her pockets full. She wishes for summer,
raspberries, her sister's hands braiding
her hair: wild thoughts meant to still
her shaking. She opens her mouth to sing
but words won't come, counts backward
silently from one hundred instead
as she hurries to help the Negro hiding
in the woods. She has promised, could do
no less after finding him starved and shivering
a day ago. She leans against a Winesap
to catch her breath, adjusts her father's
worn boots clutched under her coat, the sack
of bread-heels stolen from the pie safe.
She coughs into her elbow, sniffs the air,
smells apples and a hint of snow.

Hunger

For years she saw the moon
as a dish of mashed potatoes,
clouds as the cream she scooped
from steaming milk. When geese
honked across a clear October sky,
she saw the slide of fatted birds
across his carving board.

Those years flew faster
than a flock of sixty geese.
Her egg timer hasn't dropped
a grain of sand in the two years
since he died. Yet she can't
remember how to make
her famous airy cakes.

Asked the recipe for butter frosting
she shakes her head, muttering
about stars. She's forgotten
everything except the moon,
which she peels and peels,
hoping he will grow hungry
and come home.

What to Do with a Father

Girl, you do love a man. Even little you craved
the sweat and car-grease smells coming off
your daddy's worn green Dickies, ripped
from back-crawling into boxy caves beneath
Chevies or up under the house to fix pipes
while your mama fretted about mud-stained floors
and no water pressure. Loved scabbed up
filthy knuckles scraping your baby-soft fingers,
loved getting dirty enough to rate the soiled Lava
next to Mama's pristine Dove.

You were a girl who knew what to do
with a father. Six years old, you climbed
that rickety ladder to the roof, begged to help
pry up loose shingles, to knock in nails that locked
new ones in place. At seven you asked for a tool belt
for your Chatty Cathy doll. Stood with his tipsy
friends at Dingler's gas station, hands in pockets,
wet the greasy pavement with your spit. Knee-schooched
next to him along the garden's hot sand rows,
drowning cabbage loopers in Campbell's soup cans
of unlit gasoline. Saturdays you slouched
against him while he watched Elvis, John Wayne,
Audie Murphy. You loved that singing cowboy
because your daddy did. Cried when Elvis
limped into the desert to die, because even young
you couldn't stand to see a man look so defeated.

Stan Absher

We Last as Long as the Dew
Basho's Story, 1684

A bird from out of nowhere
flew from sky to earth, to shrub,
to a bushy maple. I kept
to the path that wound
between trees and looped

around the maple, almost
rejoining itself. I read
as I walked, from line to line
looping and darting
to follow the images

that flitted and called.
Like the bird they chirped
a language from out
of nowhere, one I longed to know
above all things. When we came

to a river, the bird vanished,
leaving behind a sobbing
child, a two year old
cast away on the roaring
river of the world.

I flung food at him and ran.
I gave him nothing, but walked away,
soothing myself with the cheeping
book. I tossed him by the foot
into the river. I sold him

on the street. I said the village
should take him in. My life is mine,
I said, to wander with book and pen
till I am their master. Hc is many,
I said, and I am one.

Winter Beeches

When cold sun sifts down through the understory,
the beech leaves glow, like a brown-winged miller
that hovers round the street lamp and beats the powder
from its wings. This light is the modest glory
of our winter. On work days, when we speed
distracted here and there, we may not notice.
But walk near in the fog, half-past the solstice—
in February, when peepers start to breed—
and light will draw us through the backlit haze
into an ashen spring. Now I think of this
half light in summer's final heat. Joe-pye's
pink clouds smolder in the ditch and days
are growing shorter; the lake's cool mist
clings to the pines -and mutes the sun's slow rise.

A Day in the Life

morning

what the setting moon
leaves behind
white stones in the river

noon

crow caws in the cedar
I am not
who I thought I was

night

all night
my door is open
only the dark breaks in

I Close My Accounts

The solstice nears. Slush of old snow funds
the Yadkin with dirty commerce. Clay banks
dictate their depositions to the river.
The river is not satisfied. I write

over each doorway in the house
I'm sorry. I'm sorry. The flamboyance
is for myself, to show God I really
suffer. What is it I've forgotten?

I begin the last words on my pad:
I rise with dawn and feel like hell.
Voices in my head, voices among
the waking birds, 'Come and see,

a bushel of barley for a penny.'
They led me like a child through court
to testify against my kind, my friends
from childhood. I did it for my children,

to look them in the eye. As my sole
bargaining chip with God. I've blazed all
the lintels with black magic marker,
but the angel will not pass over.

Pill bottles by the bed, in the library
a rack of guns. But this is how it ought
to end: Like cut grass, blanched. Like morning glory
shriveling to a pin. What will the milk cow do?

Go on chewing what she has chewed before,
her milk vein swelling to feed her bag.
Cast into the fire, I will smoke like fat.
The world we love will go on being the world.

The Boar

The boar that rooted up the vines,
and wallowed among the nodding reeds,
whose tusks slashed the olive trees
    and put sheepdogs to flight—

Xenophilus fought it with the sword
by the river where he found it, teeth
snapping, razorback bristling, breath
    smoking like burning wood,

and on an oak he hung the hide.

Paulus Silentiarius
(Greek Anthology, Book VI, 168)

Titmouse

Little heart, you endure
the cold days of the years,
life's tender lantern
perched on a tree in tears.

Through your thick plumage I see
the fire that gives you light.
Mine, though hidden by fog,
will also outlast the night.

In vain the snow crusts over.
Does it fear the morning?
But we will know joy tomorrow,
protected by our burning.

After "Mésange," a French poem by
Rainer Maria Rilke,

Asha Gowan

Fireflies, Flying Their Fire

Fireflies, at death's paling, throw stars into shadows,
Torch the night, chastise its lullaby for stealing light, and away
Flying their fire, at death's ailing, to rave at grave jars of mad glows.

I could say, have me die in my sleep, resign my life to sad woes
But my light was borne of blazing gleam, sing me back into dream the way
Fireflies, at death's paling, throw stars into shadows.

Scar the darkness, char this living's starkness, by burning glad blows.
Men, small lightning thieves, must dare brandish their flames into the dying gray,
Flying their fire, at death's ailing, to rave at grave jars of mad glows.

A wicked game of smothering life does some demon child, clad in throes,
Make when twisting the lid airtight? Maybe so, but my dreams alight to follow stray
Fireflies, at death's paling, throw stars into shadows.

Oh the pain of stolen light, and pain greater still when slow stolen! Had those
Dreams and I flown into this mortal quarantine, tied! But they glow into the gray,
Flying their fire, at death's ailing, to rave at grave jars of mad glows.

And I, once light bearer, know the torch will wane into the night, in bad pose
Of trembling gleam but dreams, living's darkness, yes dreams do betray --
Fireflies, at death's paling, throw stars into shadows,
Flying their fire, at death's ailing, to rave at grave jars of mad glows.

In Those Small Silences

Nobody ever heard my sobbing in the small silences
of my voice, thinning through the smallest echoes finding

absences in corners of my mouth that everybody saw straining
appropriately for gesturing a greeting…

but the struggle has never been far enough to ever be convincing enough
to convey enough of happy in a smile.

I must admit, as I warily greet the somebody in the mirror,
it does appear strangely beneath my dreary eyes as would something faulty I
attempted to piece or string together or weave

In a time when light left me only in darkness' scarcity
And left me to grieve while lonely.

If anybody can hear sobbing in those small silences
where absences appear in a smile,
set out to find the child.

She weeps upon the closet floor.

Indigo Child

Behind blue nightshades, the Indigo Child suffers
a bedeviling hex from the Moon that mangles his spine.

He must dissipate his skin by dint of fracture as bonesetter
for breaking the broken in his own hunkered blades.

His shaky columns exposed and heart doubled over -
he came to bare, to compose his wounds prayerfully,

"God may be seeding wings tonight."

If he cannot extract their tines, deafening Furies
will wolf down his spirit's gilded wares and bellow
his remains into ashen wisps, as would elegies tell
the death of Orestes at sunrise.

So the boy poet authors his ravages and

slithers out bad spirits before his desk
for the bludgeoning of his pen.

I felt his wings in the mist,

The Indigo Child who fiddles folklore and myths
beneath his bloodied fingertips before darkness fades,
for something to show come morning, though,
Blue behind nightshades.

The Queen's Gambit

Suitors can only guess at her frilly challis askance –
"This lady's a jest." She toys with the best,
dilly-dallies in dance, tarries romance
across the checkered game for play,
coy as to her aim,
ever clever.

Bishops bow their stance, though confess –
"This lady's distress." The marriage annuity
collects dust in the treasurer's chest while
she dosey-do's with men so vexed,
who, for Knights entitled,
would fashion themselves.

Angered and forestalled, they make
brazen bets beneath
their tantrum squalls:
"Her hand, I shall win
if nothing else!"

Fools, pawn off!
She means only to take leave
of her kingdom's castles to dance
through war and enemy battles
into arms of her King through
frontlines on the other side,

forever to sever her ties if need be
and suffer the stake of disloyalty
should their union be so,

in earnest of love's
namesake,

and away she stows.

No nobleman will solve the riddles of her
chess and though, when befuddled,
a man cannot stand it,
she cannot be deciphered –

Queen, quiet victor prevailing
in secret of her gambit.

Highwaymen crooks, brigands,
and thieves ravening run the gamut
of treachery and will surely scheme sabotage
as they behold the diadems of her royalty
and assume she is a trove of wealth
when they espy her wedding corsage,

pledged to him for whom she would die
and traipse the bullets' ambit
to brave the barrage.

Caveat emptor! Pillagers beware, she'll brandish
a blade of quicksilver so fast
not a word you'll speak of a prayer.

She'll boast her deft
wield upon the head of any double-crosser
who would beg trouble and dare steal
from the sanctity of her coffer.

Into enemy territory, she betrays and cuts
the infantry at the knees. A woman on a mission, they say,
is a formidable warrior: make no mistake,
when she waves her sword,
she hits her mark to exact sure death
– she is mighty when she slays.

Make way for the Queen who seeks
to be with her chosen One, the King, in checkmate,
to embrace and fall upon his glinting breastplate,
to dance together dazzling all who should spectate:
love forgets war and would rather twine ally and foe,

enchanting one another,
toe to toe.

And this, the lady knows:

Every stratagem is at her disposal,
every move is her grace and only One
makes her total.

No nobleman will solve the riddles of her
chess and though, when befuddled,
a man cannot stand it,
she cannot be deciphered –

Queen, quiet victor prevailing
in secret of her gambit.

King, silent man smiling,
The ring has landed.

Beneath Clouds of Sugared Hue

Like birds atop a silo's crest
stargazing during day,
I dream downy soft in you and
wander through memories
we never shared of us
running through auburn fields
to flag down the only bus
making for the city.

Sure, I could easily pick up
and leave the sameness of these dusky
dwellings but I'd rather stay here
with dreams of you than fly away
and lose memory of this place,
warm in fields of a countryside
where we could have laughed away
beneath clouds of sugared hue,
barley high, and sky blue.

Requiem of Ghosts and D Minor

In loving memory of Vincent van Gogh

Ligature confuses in his limbs
to tangle him despondent,
disarming into a stagnant tendency
stooped over a wicker chair,
saddle-sore of limp and spiritless.

Exposing the nape of his neck
to defeat's bladed guillotine,
his is a daggered soul, a fading self
realizing life was hospice
and despite a tempest wrath,
he relents a fraught thrash
to thresh a closing, instead.
Fingers shove into pigment beds
supposing one last exertion.

Painting frenzy, alla prima,
privy to musical ciphers
in tablature on the canvas,
circling desperate
to violin his sinews a requiem
of notes akin to color
wheeling tonalities

Breath dragged out to death is not long.

Like a starved vulture
drools his jowls for carcass red,
he stalks the wheat in fields, gristmills in eyes
steely to grind out their yellows.

So he trails shadows after gabbling crows,
"they fly words in my last letter to Theo"
and in his fist, he rams the palette knife
into the stretched cloth to draw the shade
out of feathers thundering nigh,

all but for the kiss of
some heavenly reminiscence,

shy of illusion, grant him a vision

beyond some simple memory peer.

Oh, but that road is dead-ended,
cut off as a path terse
because travelers prefer ones that make
not for too winded. Even at touch upon his lost ear,
his heart anguishing for a world that doesn't
care to hear in melodies is still beating him there.

Gun pointed to the chest, he pulled the trigger,
the blessed bullet that crashed through the cage
binding him came to halt the agony of ill vigor.

But his ghost, I believe, still stares into the wheat
where they found him.

Van Gogh's phantom grapples immortal
to oust evils of society ever here to aggrieve
the sanctity of the Pure,

returning to assure this Saintly Quality
is to be equally seen in peasant,
field of wheat, valley mead,
and in those jilted lovers
who deplete their spirit's well-being
forever more for truths they breathe of Beauty.

"Sorrow's mock was my forced monkhood
I, indentured to a lapidary sky, was
ordered celibate from any real contact,
trencher shoveling out tears of cry,
destined to be no good, and thought ill of
if not to graft a smile and wax contented
as an artist should.

But mankind's hypocrisies
and false virtues were of hues
I could not match resemblance to.

I wish they would only take me as I am."

Vivekanand Jha

An Epistle to Poem

Dear poem!
What do I state? Where do I begin from?
Trial and strife trails me like a slash
since the day you made your way in my life.

Truth's a bit, not easy to conceive
and convince. While I remain drowned
configuring you a form and figure,
decking you with a cloak
of rhyme, rhythm and metre.

But my wife and so-called friends
nursing a grudge against me,
I overhear them murmuring
of sudden change in my chemistry.

They notice in me
a sudden surge of arrogance
as safe distance now I prefer
where once, an active participant.

I feel affronted when I find you
stranded in uproar and tumult,
someone playing a spiteful joke
with your chastity, doing prose
and calling you poetry.

Your company I never thought
in the jerks and jolts of an odyssey.
I know I alone am not your fan
already adorned by many a man.

This, an age of fabrication,
of machine. Trusting someone
is like the sunrise from the west
and the sun-set in the east.

I don't know for how long
this love is to last. I gave up

brooding, bemoaning the future
as I want to live an age in a moment.

My wife calls it a mere flirt,
as fleeting as the heaving of a sigh,
boding peril of the love-lorn,
warning me, my dropping down
around her and pooling at her feet:
One morning to mourn.

Tolerance

No one to help in scaling the ladder
but many to dislodge its rungs,
waiting in obsession
for its feet to slither on the ground
splashed with the grease of envy.

Unmindful of these vampires
nourished on the blood of brutality
my father - innocuous and euphemistic -
sermonizes only verse of tolerance,
adept in the chemistry of words
and teaches me how to be a catalyst.

He hardly knows the geometry of words
like a satire, pun, irony, oblique, etc.
but what he knows
potent enough outfoxing all
and his counsel I follow
like a suffocating man gasping for air:

"Give up the life tinged with tussle,
draw a line, parallel and longer,
by the one your rival draws.
Thus culminates the road to rivalry
delivered by the womb of jealousy."

Bruised Land

This land of ominous geography,
calamities cuddle in its lap
drenched in disease and destitution.
It dies its left-over death
amid flip-flop of deluge and drought.

Habitats break into fleeting ocean,
the destiny of the people floating
over the surging current of water
as if they were exposed to
venomous sting of cobra.

Everyone on board the same boat
the stream underneath is pointed enough
to peg a hole in the hull and keel.

Thatched roof - the only cloak of privacy,
animals – only livelihood for the peasants,
are swept away as if
they were a bobbing boat of paper.

They come as usual
with a script of concocted speech
to assess the damage and crisis
and assure: we are looking to work it out
on a permanent basis. But nothing happens
after they return to their cocoon,
breathing a sigh in the bonnet of bun.

Talking big is their dogma;
chanting through flowery, glib tongue
and adoring the public on the altar
of betrayal their worship.
Whoring people with pre-poll-pledges
All they do in the realm of charlatanism.

Scapegoat

Ceremonious knives lastly dropped
on disinterested and innocent animals
much like their falling on cakes
as men dipped in delusion, swear
to sacrifice them on the altar
betokening fulfillment of their dream:

Their demands stretching wide
like a canopy of the sky,
ranging without any beginning and end.
Sometimes they leave to His discretion
Sometimes they go on to demand:

"How should I beseech?" They muse,
"Omniscient and omnipresent You are,
You know what is hidden
in the inner core of my heart.

But You have to listen, look after all,
lest You forget me by mistake
so I swear to sacrifice a goat
in Your pious premise
upon fulfillment of my wishes and desires.

Today exam-result has come out,
my friend stands first in the class.
Now he has to translate the promise into action:
Champagne, roasted chicken and mutton
would be served and spoilt in celebration.

It's marriage of another friend of mine,
Things are set to meet and greet;
club, restaurant and bar booked,
one night fish and the next day meat.

These are only a small roster of atrocities
Wherever or whenever music of celebration
transmits and whispers into animals' ears,
they get heavily loaded with doubt and fear:
Only God knows whose turn next;
and who would watch and mourn.

Toxin-Tipped Words

Our politicians, merchants
of vibrant, electoral democracy
are cultivating a novel poll weapon
of toxin-tipped words,
flooding the lexis with new entrants
of vices and venoms.

It's not the first time; new thing,
only medium of discourse has changed.
We can understand their disquiet,
sudden harmonic imbalances and fear.
The festival of fleece near,
They rehearse to chant the satanic verse
seeking salvation for selves
spitting befooling words.

The new gutter dialogue,
carries limitless sewage,
stinking a rotten egg-like smell,
words leaving their tongues
as aimless as the boat
without oars and rudder.

A pompous journey on a felonious fling,
through the sewers of language,
setting the course of the nation to capsize
into the water woes of hazy politics.

Deborah Hall

Owl Part 1-5

Spring

Now, naked stand the trees against an ocean canopy of sky,...
creaking the burdened song of a history of heavy snows,
their outstretched limbs reaching....straining...to touch the clouds
that ride upon the backs of forsaken Gods....
Will Hades, the Toll-Taking Angel, return the favor of their song,
releasing his summer Mistress from the Dark months,
so to hold captive the frozen earth? Warming his feet with her heat?
Quiet and crying, in silence at the corner of the north facing room,
rattling chains are heard unlocking the door, the Debutant cascades
down the stairs in a gown dressed in the stars of Aquarius and Pisces,
smelling of distant fires..... as an Owl who is equipped
to take authority over the night..
for a while she will be the smile of the Moon...

Owl

Granite trees shown,,, she flew... alone… through those magnet branches
Chasing the calls of tiny chances...
she flew
through a child's night of endless black water skies
the man in the moon looking down on her with his one Cyclops's eye
Winking knowingly.....
Upon those cellophane wings she flew
a mouthful of stars singing a night music of blue
A cure for the day...lifting her up on laughter
she flies
UP and Away....

Blood

My Blood is in this Place, one drop at a time with no holding back….
I saw it on those starched white sheets of that hospital bed,
"is that all from me?"

Yes, they said…

no expression…

the color of the Blood Moon on an October eve, 2014
A check in with the universe…a color to be respected for a reason
But I have given it so many times…should it be a surprise?
only now its mark makes itself known, of a measure on those endless white clouds
of my hospital sheets…..

Yes,
that is me spilled out,

Yes….
this is me. I was once here…

Ghosts

She traveled where the winds would take her
Along the dusty trail of a tangled tumbleweed
Those hitchhikers, the faces of her ancestry, smiling down
Or up as it may go…walking the barren roads of a dismal day
…..skeptical of finding a summer road
Could this be it?
Paper maps dissolve in the acid rain…a gnarled finger points the way
telling the story of a full moon on a West Indies night....
Summer, Winter, Spring and Fall in an aging face of knowing eyes
Holding onto the Life of those that speak in flickers of a candle….

Wings

The wings he pointed out
are the most delicate...
but are able to withstand the strongest of winds;
bearing the weight over many miles....
Push... glide... soar, a rhythm beats above a coral sea, in and out of a paradise lost
to man
this coat of mist colored jewels is worn proudly,
a gift from the ancient volcanoes
passed over...
The call to fly is the command,
Night passes through the day....as sunset once again tenderly touches searching
lips
Driving the eternal thirst for a drink of the fresh dew of dawn
Outstretched wings touch clouds of pink
Flying over sailing ships
I see you there......

Robert Okaji

What Edges Hold

By which I mean those lines framed in certainty: the demarcation of sunlight and shadow. Kami signifies not spirit, but rather that force above man.

Never religion, but life itself: the mountains, trees, the rocks. Lightning.

Or waves, thundering off the coast, lured by the moon.

Stirring the water with a spear, Izanagi dripped an island into being.
Separate the ordinary through limitation, by practice, by ritual and space.

Another night in the twisted trees. The god-shelf.

Recognize that wind respects no borders.

Knowing that to the east questions may respond to answers I have long suspected, I look elsewhere. After the vowel, the consonant.

Though torii differ in style, each retains two posts and a crosspiece.

After the consonant, the winnowed tunnel, extinguished light.

At the gate, bow respectfully, then enter. Ladle water from right to left, then left to right. Pour it into your left hand, then cleanse your mouth.

Invert and regard the precipice.

I have placed one foot in their sphere. The other still searches.

Ritual

Placing the dead is seldom arbitrary.
The Marquis de Sade's grave in the forest at Malmaison
was planted with acorns so that he might be consumed by
trees, but my wife desires a shady plot in rural Texas,
where no one will claim her. In old Christian
graveyards the unclean were buried at the gospel side for

sinners. When her best friend died, she and his former lover
split a bottle of Johnny Walker Black and listened to Puccini.
The Nuer of Sudan place deformed dead babies by the river,
returning them to their true fathers, the hippos. After the fog
crushed Stevie Ray's helicopter, I played *Texas Flood* on the juke
box and quit my job. In China, bones channel *feng shui*, becoming
part of the active landscape. Though she wanted her ashes to drift
in the Pacific, my mother's body lies in a national cemetery in
San Antonio. On the northwest coast of Canada, the Kwakiutl
left their dead to the ravens, and my father has proposed
on numerous occasions that we shove a hambone up his ass
and let the dogs drag him off. I do not believe we'll follow his
suggestion. In old England, suicides were often interred at
crossroads, impaled, to impede their restless wandering spirits.
The Torajans sometimes keep bodies wrapped in layers of absorbent
cloth in their homes for years. I'd like my incinerated, pulverized
remains released in the jet stream, if only to escape economy class for
once. Jellyroll Morton's grave is in Section N, Lot 347, #4, in the northwest
quadrant of Calvary Cemetery, but some villagers bury stillborn
near a dwelling's outer wall. Hugh Hefner is rumored to have acquired
the spot next to Marilyn Monroe. Placing the dead is never arbitrary.

With These Nine Figures

... and with the sign 0...any number may be written.
Leonardo of Pisa (Fibonacci)

We attain from emptiness and the Sanskrit *shoonya*, from *safira* and *sifr,* zero.
As in unoccupied, as in void, as in what brims the homeland of null.
I once counted thirty-four black vultures orbiting my neighbor's hill.
Despite appearing in Mayan codices, they neither sing nor cipher.
Fibonacci's *Book of the Abacus* introduced the decimal system to Europe.
Regarding the tyranny of mathematics, is nothing something?
From alterity to belonging, its provenance assumes an absence of being.
Which is not to suggest xenophobia or superiority in order.
Whether depicted by empty space, wedges, or hooks, it held place.
Representation not of the object, but of its purpose, its path.
Black vultures do not smell carrion, but pillage from those that can.
Obliterative in the west wind, subtractive, unbound, they spiral.
Are the circlers in the sky symptomatic or merely symbolic?
Comparing negative infinity to its positive sister, I observe their way.

Letter from Austin

Michael, when you say moons do you see
cold stone floating in the firmament
or phrases frayed in the mouth and spat on paper?
And does the Spanish moon simmer at a similar
pace to mine or yours? Which embers blush brighter?
But let's turn to estuaries, to salt and clamor and gun-
running poets and interrupted words sold in stalls
between parenthetical gates, to incomparable cavas
and the deterioration of envy and intervening years.
Or perhaps mislaid passion – a friend claims love
is merely a bad rash, that we scratch and scratch
and inflame but never truly cure what ails us. Sounds like
politics to me. Or sports. And business. Or neighborhoods.
On my street people should cook and play music together,
laugh, raise chickens and read good books. They should
brew beer, swap tomatoes, recite each other's poetry and sing
in tune. But we're different here, preferring instead electronics
glowing in dimly lighted rooms. I reject this failure, as I also
reject the theory of centrifugal force spinning off the moon's
body from the earth's crust, preferring to imagine a giant
impact blasting matter into orbit around what morphed into the
earth, and somehow accreting the stuff into this orb we
sometimes worship. This, to me, is how good relationships
form: explosions of thought and emotion followed by periods
of accretion. But what I mean is I hope this finds you well
by the river of holy sacrament. Remember: brackish water
bisects our worlds. Turn. Filter. Embrace. Gotta run. Bob.

Rice

Yesterday's rain informs me I'm born of luck and blended
strands, of hope and words forged before a common tongue emerged.

Of my first two languages only one still breathes.

The other manifests in exile, in blurred images and hummed tunes.

Rice is my staple. I eat it without regarding its English etymology,
its transition from Sanskrit to Persian and Greek, to Latin, to French.

Flooding is not mandatory in cultivation, but requires less effort.

Rice contains arsenic, yet I crave its polished grains.

In my monolingual home we still call it *gohan*, literally cooked rice, or meal.
The *kanji* character, *bei*, also means America.

Representing a field, it symbolizes abundance, security, and fertility.

Three rice plants tied with a rope. Many. Life's foundation.

To understand Japan, look to rice. To appreciate breadth, think *gohan*.
Humility exemplified: *sake* consists of rice, water and mold.

The words we shape predicate a communion of aesthetics.

Miscomprehension inhabits consequence.

Dianne DeCaire

Matching Halos

I loved you badly
I loved them all badly
they loved it though and they
called the radio and dedicated me to moons
and moons to me
moons around Jupiter
or whatever planet that was
the fashion of the day
we wore matching halos silly us so in love
believing like that is magic
that silly word I mean magic
these are the strong emotions that we
turn around and beat
with a stick
all our lives until the blood flows in rivulets
until it flows from altars of love
until it turns to catsup [not wine!]
surprise surprise
at the sour vinegary thing I
have turned into

It's gonna Pop now

He's away now
I can clear out my head
the unbleached
muslin curtains flutter in delight
new scents enter through the open
window
French violets [French perfume!]
please my peace is so lovely please
wrap me in your arms wrap me in a curtain like a
chrysalis
the milkweed pods are gonna pop now
the silken threads will float all around me
in a shining halo
He's away I'm away oh how far I can go
I float away on the milkweed so soft

he will wonder where I have gone now
he will not think to look up
look up so very
high
as I am able to reach

That Same Old Formula

Things that are at once different
and the same
different
the same
a photo that reminds you
of the you that
scrumbled paint across new worlds
unfurled into womanhood
so boldly so blunderingly
and then wore a hood to hide her sex
the candles are burning low low low
blow no don't blow
sh shhh don't breathe now don't bother the flame
light a new one or two or seven or maybe just
eat that whole bag of cookies what
the hell [!]
yes it is all just the same in a way
I always think I'm all brand new and then
see that same old formula
written in ink
fading black bitter ink
on the plaster cracked wall
the only one I really understand

Angelaurelio Soldi

Trilogy

The history of our tribes

There was the land rich with milk and honey
besotted we took it
the one you used
the one you did not use
fructified in our hands
in our bosoms.
You complain it is your land.
who doesn't know the history
of our tribes? Yours, ours.
The rocks of Judea and Samaria
were foundations
long before we left for lives
encumbered with memories
bond to a covenant.
We are back we cannot help it.
If we take the water
you say it is your water too
but it flows just the same for us
it moistens our tongues
as we husband it.

We have taken away your hopes
your prayers. We learned long ago
not to trust anybody.
You are enraged for your heart is heavy.
Why should we give back anything
when we know you won't be grateful
nor will you be satisfied?
We were never satisfied.
The river flows where it cuts its bed
nothing does its work for him
who would do ours?
You live behind the walls we have erected
the way we have lived before.
We have no choice our hearts are set
we know the misery of being on the other side.
Prisoners of our loves
our hates our fears our needs our alikeness

our destinations are the same
always and inevitably the same
we can't be but what we are
nor can we choose how we are.

God willing

How can I keep my brother from killing you?
You build on the ruins of his hopes.
And how can I keep my sons
their blood boils under your humiliations.
Why do you blow up their houses?
You do not blow up the houses of your children
when they murder
and my land is soaked with blood
you spilled.
Why should I do any less?
The sun has risen on these lands
for my father and for the fathers of his father
here we gathered our harvests
as long as we can remember
and our words are written on the walls on the stones
in the lands you occupy.
You can't erase them.
We have pastured Abraham's sheep
for he is in our bosoms
and God willing
we will have again our trees.

Only the land knows

Year after year
every year
we long for renewal.
The sun warm on our shoulders
at home in the towns
on the hills and the fields
the road open and everyone free
the labors rewording.
Year after year
till the last year.
But the soul grows its prejudices
the mind fabricates their defenses
and the heart grows savage
while the land becomes a prison.
We fell threatened
we fell outrage
and all hearts grow more savage
and the land weighs and patiently records
all the losses.
Only the land knows what it bears
waiting for peace.

Yeon-seong Park

Chun-Hyang's Yard

There she recalled the smells of days long past
the yellow earth,
dark brown jars,
holding soybean sauce and red-bean paste.
In a place like this
the kitchen maid made a wood fire
and cooked rice.

Her father never dreamt of
the days when his youngest daughter
would stand in the yard of St. Catherine's.

He often said
"Girls are girls.
They will get married,
and give a birth to a kid
with another name."
He did not care much about her progress.

But it was his daughter
who flew to Cambridge
and talked with people from many countries.

She has to admit
that he did pay for this
out of savings
another father
might have given to a son.

Now her father is in his 80's,
and silver streaks her hair, too.
But she is a victor today.
Her friend flew
from Honolulu
and they stood together
in the yard of Chun-hyang.

Like a Picnic

We step out of the school,
which cages students
until night is deep.
We wear school uniforms,
white cotton blouses and
black flannel skirts.
When we board bus number 6,
passengers' heads turn toward us,
wondering why
we are here during school time.

As the bus moves out of the city
cosmos bloom in white and blue
on either side of the road, and
rice fields lie quiet
in the autumn sun.

Though someone is dead,
the house is not much crowded.
In the yard,
only a few women come and go
holding a small table of rice wine
to serve the guests.
My friend appears,
in hemp clothes.
Her lips go upward a little
when she finds us.

Before the picture of her dead father
we stand in a row.
Our teacher picks
a long, green stick of juniper,
and burns it.
The white smoke of incense
sends out the smell of a forest.

While we bow together,
the wailing sound of a mourner
breaks the silence.
It rises and falls
so rhythmic and so sudden
that I bite my lips and tighten my shoulder.

Red Fruit

Who wants this one?
Long time ago in Palestine,
The red nectar from the fruit
quenched
the thirst of Herodia.

It happened again
in the hand of a man
in black
holding the fruit incarnated up to
the glare of media light.

Behind its shadow
Towers falling
soldiers dying in the sandstorms
prisoners tortured in the brutal camp
oil factories burning

We have witnessed this fruit
far too long;
Now
is the time for
a mutation.

Cobweb Castle

Out of her finger tips
grows the cobweb.
She builds the castle with it.

Is it a delicate look of the castle or
its esoteric scent
that attracts people?

Not a few knights, peasants, or kings
have contrived
their own excuses to visit.

The moment they enter the castle

the castle suddenly
becomes a mirage,

transparent and fleeting —
leaving them puzzled,
empty-handed.

Dandelion Blues

That cold spring
When delicate dandelions started
to bloom,
His action of taking his life
as an adjunct professor,
Leaving
His last will and testament
To the president of Korea,
That action was his last word
to the unconcerned to unjust situations.
For a while
Pens and microphones
Carried his desperate gesture
like busy bees.

Grave faces placed incense sticks
in the burner
but they left,
in twos and threes,
before the sticks burnt to ashes.

Future

With gems and pebbles
in both pockets
Still we are waiting for
hidden revelation.
So the job of a photographer,
a thirst for discovering
a ravishing pattern,
making our heart
leap up.

Arnold Johanson

How I Came to Be a Poet

Blocks. Wooden shapes in many colors,
mostly red, lined up, piled and angled
to fashion precarious structures:
houses, barns, garages, churches, cages.
Homes for monkeys, horses, cars, baby Jesus
and little plastic GIs with guns and bayonets.
They'd last until a cat tail, sibling toe,
or the laws of physics
did them in.

Then came blocks with big bold letters
to spell out CAT, DOG, GOD, DAM, MAD
followed by tablets, pencils, and scads
of words to play with, to make whatever
my imagination could contrive.

That play goes on, building towers and fortresses
with nouns and verbs, slyly adding adjectives for color
and décor. No more fear of cats with angry tails.
They do show up, when I want them. But a twist
of my wrist can take a hissy calico and turn her
into a buxom blonde, a commando with a bayonet,
or even baby Jesus.

another day . . .

A lot of history's gone down
in the lives of two old men
in wheelchairs and pajamas
eating Salisbury steak, mashed potatoes,
ginger cake and applesauce.
They stare and grumble
at each other and at the food.

One of them made a living
dancing marathons in the '30s.
He says the Dodgers are a cinch

to take it all this year. *I hope*
they finish in the basement
the former corporate exec
expectorates, *baseball's*
a white man's game.
"That Robinson has moves,"
the dancer answers, "like Nijinsky.
He and Pee Wee are the best combo . . ."
they're a couple of fags
the businessman butts in.

Every meal's the same: sports and politics,
race and sex. Sometimes they check
the newspapers to document their point
but never can remember what they're looking for
and anyway, those idiot papers
can't even get the year right.

Eastern Box Turtle

I went out to get the paper, damn near tripped
on a turtle in the middle of our driveway.
I tried to chat him up, but he kept his head
inside his carapace, disinclined
to talk, or to move.

I call him "he," though I really didn't check.
Males, I've learned, have concave plastrons
but I wouldn't know a plastron if I saw one
and I didn't want to pick him up. The golden rule
applies. I would not be pleased if some humungous lunk
picked up my house with me inside, to examine
my plastron and other parts, to set me down again
willy-nilly; or, God forbid, to drop me in a cauldron
of chicken stock with garlic, onions, tomato and thyme.

I fear this forest-dwelling reptile's land, and maybe family,
have fallen prey to the developers who turned
the forty-acre wood behind our house into red clay desert.
I'd have loved to help him find new digs, but was content
to admire his five by five by five inch shell,
a Jackson Pollock blend of reds, greens and browns
with a bold array of gold. Perfect camouflage
for a forest floor of autumn leaves.

Old Dog

I chased that phony bunny round the track.
Never could get close enough to sniff her rump
so they gave me the pink slip.
Claimed I didn't have the heart or legs.
Don't need those to serve at stud I thought,
soon learned that losers don't get laid.

I got adopted, got a big back yard
to scamper in. But it's no fun to run
without a bunny. So I mostly stay
inside the house and sleep.

Sometimes when I've gotta go
I whimper and they come with leash
to lead me out. Sometimes I just let it flow
and listen to their tough-love litany:
bad boy,
            dumb dog,
                        worthless shit-for-brains.

Wake me if tomorrow brings
a world worth barking at.

Well-tempered in Leipzig

Did you ever rest, Johann Sebastian?
Constantly composing, desperate to meet
the Capellmeister cantata quota.
Did Anna Magdalena ever yell
as you headed out the door "Johann, wait!
Why not stay home this once?
We'll play a little gin, maybe drink
a little gin, then read some poetry?"

When you dragged yourself home
from a long day in the loft,
did she un-boot you, set you
in the comfy chair, gently rub
your tender feet, pour you a tall
cold one or two, hand you the *Zeitung*,
and keep the kids away until dinner?

All those kids! Their number tells us
you and Anna did more than rest
when you finally hit the sack.
Tell me, were there preludes
with your nocturnal fugues?
I did read somewhere once, I think,
that when you finally slept
you snored in E-flat minor.

Conversation with Death, July, 2014

I know, I know. It's a tough job.
Going on forever *would* get tedious
and, anyway, there isn't room.
I understand.

But could you go somewhere else
for a year or three or four?
You've reaped a rich harvest lately
from folks I love – Tom, Eleanor,
Charley, Roland. Yes, they were all old,
but you could have spaced them out a bit,
let me see them each again a time or two.
Their minds were still full-strength.

I know, you've got a lot of work to do
and yes, I could have taken time
to visit them, but I didn't know.
That's what I hate about you, dear,
you never let us know.

I often see you eye my Alice, licking
your chops. So far just a nasty tease,
like what you've done with Dave
the last few years. Are you the one
who slowly eats their bodies, drags
the process out? I used to think
you were an angel, but even fallen angels
aren't that mean.

Anyway, whenever you want me, I'll be ready.
Just stop the goddamn teasing.

Recognition

Stripes and stars in chaos on his shirt.
A black Stetson with a cluster of flags
anchored in its tri-color band.
Buttons pinned at random:
    Don't tread on me; Jesus saves;
    a backslash through an Obama caricature . . . .
a walking, stomping, chanting photo-op
at every Tea Party rally.

One of my childhood friends, perhaps.
And but for the grace of liberal professors,
unorthodox clergy, hard thinking, imagination
and a loving wife saved by similar graces,
there go I, raised to believe, like him,
in self-reliance, Jesus and the G. O. P.

I watch him exercise his right to act the fool
as he eyes folks like me, thanking his God
he isn't one of us.

The Philosopher, A Little Behind in His Thinking

I've never seen my butt.
My head and neck can't twist enough.
I could rig a mirror behind me
to reflect into the one in front of me
and show me a reflection
of an image of my rump.
But that, as Plato said,
would be a third-rate copy
of a second-rate reality.
Such an end could never
justify those means.
As Kant reminded us
even my wife,
who is privileged
to look at me rear-on,
sees only my phenomenal ass.
The thing-in-itself
is known only to God.
Sort of like the far side of the moon.

What A Little Moonlight Can Do
for Ken Eill

They call me a moldy fig.
A quiet message from the codger
who shares my Central Park bench.

His eyes tell me that right now
he's listening to Ellington,
or maybe Anita O'Day backed by Basie.

I grow uneasy as he talks on.
I don't have time for in-detail
accounts of this guy's life back
in the '30s, hanging out on 52nd St.,
sneaking into clubs or listening
through open windows in July.

> *Bumped into Billie Holiday one day. She stared*
> *and grumbled some obscenities, but softened*
> *as I sputtered my apology, then smiled, brought me in,*
> *set me at her table, ordered me a coke, added*
> *a little something from her flask,*
> *sang* What A Little Moonlight Can Do
> *just for me.*

He went off to fight the Nazis,
picked up a tenor sax in Paris,
couldn't get the hang of it,
got drunk and tossed it in the Seine.

He has, he says, maybe thirty thousand
dollars worth of vintage vinyl
he never listens to. The masters
all are jamming in his head,
no scratches, skips, or signs of age.

The moldy hepcat fig, supported
by his hand-carved walking stick,
totters off and leaves me wondering
where it was I thought I needed to be.

RuthCarlin

Natural Confetti

Natural confetti,
blossom petals, pink,
but not cherry,
strewn on the street,
lining the gutters,
softening the wrench
of loss
sweetly offering an odor
of love
no longer attached to the tree
wilting, matting,
taking on shreds of candy wrappers
and tire tracks
pinkening the cracked asphalt
leading the way
to the exit
the brief life of beauty
giving an example of beauty
so we'll know it
the next time
it catches our eye
for that one moment
of solidity
that makes sense
that seizes into alignment
heart
mind
soul
and then sneezes off
in a spring breeze

and the pieces lie
all about me
fragments
never to be refitted

oddities
curiosities
that catch sunlight
glint
distract
take your eye places
it would never go
but go it does
and sometimes the other
eye too
wanders with it
and I marvel at the remnants
that weren't my life
but clues
to something
long forgotten
or no thing
remembered

Hollow Cost

figures of sorrow
phrasing limb to limb
embedding heads
in armpits
fallen arches
sheer against
each other
ribs interlocking
interlacing
like fingers
tracing a memory
on skin parchment
no eyes
but sockets
waiting for the light

staircases
layered with bones
turning everything
you may have thought
on its side
putting to use
repurposing

the tone
heard by
no one
no two
though a constant echo
pulls you awake
puts nightmare
into your day
brings you a "you"
which might otherwise
have eluded you

so you plunk down
words
in an effort
to find a weight
to keep you here
get you here

but the earth's gravity
is not yours

Current Events

There's a hole
in my heart
shaped like an
airplane.
The blood leaks
through it,
useless fuel, dripping
into the empty pit
of my stomach.
I clutch
at the pain,
but strangely
it's outside me
casting its metal
bands around
like a cage,
I can't release it,
it's welded about
me; only, I can
peer through
its openings
at the open sky
with the memory
of freedom
which was never
freedom after all.

We belong together,
side by side,
standing for peace,
signaling harmonious
co-existence,
but for the hate
that crumpled us,
reduced us to tears
and powdery ashes.
Stand up tall
they had said
put your hand
to your heart
and then, "I pledge
allegiance to the
flag of the. . ."
But what was that?
President Kennedy
got shot and Betsy
and I made up a
chant: "the President's
dead he got shot in
the head," over and
over until we fell
asleep not to awaken
till September 11, 2001.

Bruce Lader

After a Visit from the Angel of Insomnia Relief

A trumpet's breathing this
rhythm around the heart
of how it tastes
to feel *fantabulous beyond words,*

it's a trilling tingle on the tip
of letting loose a mint of vibes
wealthier than billionaires,

breezing over the borders of reality I float
dip & split tones,
don't need a doctor,

it's a *zero-g thrust* of zesty cosmic pizza
zooming past politics & death,
a salty riff swiped
from Mulligan & Baker steaming up
Mardi Gras stew,

it's the key to Brooklyn Bridge
swinging open a gate
of light on Miracle Street, it's
remembering the lady I long to look at most
scats the sexiest
half-notes of laughter,

hungers to be with me
presto,
savor this jive-possessed guy
gone bonkers
dabbing hot-sauce sounds,
blowing blue soul
through catchy bebop chops

into the wind's buffet

When Cats Could Fly

Like snow leopards
they owned the highest vantage points

stalked the airy altitudes between alpine peaks.

They didn't have bird wings.
With webbed claws broader than a lynx's
catching breezes and gliding on moonlight

they surveyed jungle canopies perched
in treetops sometimes were mistaken for owls.

Humans ascended in hot-air balloons
for a chance to touch
their cumulous coats.

Abundant as the stars in clear sky
they'd coast from cliffs forage beaches

celebrate their independence night after night.

For games they'd swipe at turkeys
and ostriches pose the most frustrating riddles

caterwaul louder than a flock of gulls at low tide.

A few still have feral flashbacks of flying
and scratch us or snap with fishbone teeth.

Our Own Blood

The generals deliberate on the climate of war,
insulted that some harebrained foreigners
might beat them at seizing the capital.

The generals read barometers of insiders,
tally missiles and unmanned drones.
Their temperatures escalate as the budget deficit
dives and the foreigners move forward.

The Supreme Commanders would like nothing better
than to turn the tide, reduce the expense of casualties
to zero, risk only what's necessary,
leave nothing to accident.

Fingers like rolls of million-dollar bills
toying with the buttons of boom,
the generals reckon lives,
plot exact targets via satellite surveillance.

The security of our native land hovers
like Apache helicopters
on a do-or-die sortie.

The generals know it has always been
us or the enemy, the battle between
alien blood and our own.

Reverse Noir

Pre-dawn glow, fleeing to the border
both realize they've been poisoned, fatally;
she slips hand in blouse, pulls Derringer,
keep driving and don't try anything funny—
a roadblock, then blast of honk, headlights
barreling at them in the rain, he swerves
onto shoulder, precipice a stowaway.

Suspicions turn paranoid of ulterior motives
to eliminate the other, abscond with briefcase
containing antidote, possess a piece
of that elusive golden light, take it along
an unmapped road of shadowed entanglement,
a dream losers triumph, bask in a jackpot,
redeem blundered affairs, loves trifled.

If it weren't a dangerous risk to trust an exile,
his dubious resources, her covert contacts,
they'd split the loot, wallow in happiness
at the husband's expense in exotic settings
beyond the law, have a foolproof racket
devised on a nifty scheme with the traveler
whose lonely craving flesh duped him.

He wagered his last dollar she was hooked
all the way down when she had *him*
in her palm, took the enthralled pigeon
for a ride head over heels in a lair of hungry
promises, reneged with counterfeit talk,
the net of deceit dropped, every link
tightened on the drifter desperate for a job

in a town tyrannized by the husband,
a wire-pulling lothario jealous of the world,
aloof from the spell-binding woman
who endorses a deal with the wanderer,
treats him to a salad bar and movie,
sidles over in a bookshop, plants a seed
of intrigue that germinates a dilemma.

Priscilla McCelvey

Ars Poetica

Look for the world in the corners of spice cabinets, the edges of salty wooden
piers.

Uncover soaked marsh leaves, get mud on the sides of calves, find quarters
or delicately torn candy wrappers, maybe even a turtle shell.

Admire bark-scraped knees as earned wounds.

Analyze the flaked rust in an old tea kettle.

Note the curves of bananas.

Cultivate these images until they're tangled vines on your cerebrum, aching
to be pulled apart.

Keep picturing your beloved's features with the chord changes of your favorite
song.

Understand how knowledge can haunt, but use it to fine-tune the sunburned
memory
of the grit between your toes

when the beach still felt new, and spring was a blessing,

not part of a giant cycle
where you're a buzzing insect.

Hold these fragments close, wait for the trigger
to fill fragile pages with smudged ink:

rest, you, unpublished, crisply bound thing, on an old creaky shelf,
with your corners that yearn
to be touched.

To My Wish List, Age 17

You sought an expansive collection of teacups
cradling dried flowers, and a map covered in

neon thumbtacks. You sought a snug library heaving
with must, you sought castles with big ol' grand pianos,

you sought footfalls in faraway places with no one's hand like
stone in your pocket. This is before you were all walls and boxes,

and your wish to be a traveling breeze came true.
This is before you found out the painting elephants

that calmed you might have been beaten,
and before you learned your landlocked body

would do anything to just escape your frenzied brain.
You sought to know the sound of whale heartbreak

and to dream in black and white, but this was before
you realized how naïve these little fancies were –

now you must always carry the curse to wander,
as the rattle of your brain repents and prays to the wind.

The anywhere but here song

It's like being forced to sleep
in a gas station bathroom,
cockroaches nibbling my sleeve.

No, it's like the feeling of being
stuck under a muddy porch
with mosquitoes for the night

after you stripped me raw, the sweet
lies you fed me summon piercing
bug snouts like fangs, but your

barbed-wire growl wrapped around my wrist,
"Don't move." Or – like you mailed me
off to a far-away slaughterhouse

so I could witness its cement insides
and learn not to shudder and dizzy while
slicers and dicers spatter me with blood.

It's like I am here, I am now, I'm with you
in your arms, cowering, uttering the lie of
"I love you," murmuring how I'll stay.

Even the hill tribes have satellite TV now[1]

We're almost born to press click. We rely
on the florescent, the first buzz in the morning.

We constantly look down, losing the ability to look far off
into the distance, as if the textures of trees in the park,

the fuzzy contrast between mountain and sky, and the wave
from a friend down the street don't deserve the attention we pay

to the zoom, to the flash, to the likes of our precious virtual lives.
We adorn the metallic squares in our pockets like temples,

throwing dollars to the same people who kill the earth with plastic.
Now, there is an island in the ocean, made from garbage soup

the size of two Texases, that inhales the seawater, while we eschew
the air when we talk to each other. We have become filtered.

We have become deliriously artificial. We with our tangled piles
of headphones, our photos gone in ten seconds, our worth

determined by cyberspace. We are fueled by the thing polluting us.
It only takes seven minutes of nature to sooth our racing minds,

---

[1] Based on "a rake's progress"
archaic English, phrase
1. Progressive deterioration, especially due to self-indulgence
2. Based on a series of paintings by William Hogarth, 1735, telling the story of Tom Rakewell, a man who turns to vice after inheriting money from his father

but there I go finding solace in image searches of exotic places,
in hashtags and Pinterest boards. I can't even meditate without an app

to guide my dandelion-whisker-thoughts. Once, I saw a tribal village.
They lived off of the land with ads for watery beer plastered

on their planked homes. They used elephants for farming.
They had roofs made from palm fronds, and the children's soccer ball

was a water bottle. But then the blare of the makeshift generator
for the TV during the mid-afternoon nap, and the children abandoning

their soccer game to beg for the privilege of taking selfies. And I let them,
those not-yet-so-crooked hopefuls with their farsight still intact,

their posing uncultivated, they who clutch to our castoffs and teach us
how not to need. That night, we all went home to our flashing screens.

When I rode the train through the projects

It was summer again on the crisis hotline.
It was tales of the projects like ghosts
in the fabrics of my clothes. It was ghosts
hiding in vines covering the swing-sets, in shards
of glass like knives near the train tracks, half-bricks

crumbling out of houses. It was ghosts
nibbling at security blankets. It was curling
up in a small glass room. It was meth addicts,
slouching zombies in the summer heat.
It was stories following me home, the whispers

pressing against swollen cheeks, slicing open
tear ducts: if I don't get taken off the Section 8 list
where will my baby sleep – nowhere to go – I can't sleep –
my nephew's abused, they keep him in closets --
looking over my shoulder because of noises in the night—

bruises above ribs –I got followed to work today –
my husband beats me if I try to leave him –
someone knocked on my windshield at a red light –
help me, I can't feed my baby, I can't pay my bills,
I can't stop crying – me neither – I want this to end –

me, too. It was shouldering their histories.
It was giving callers' places to go, hope – I *had* to hope –
that their problems would be fixed. It was a collage
of what-should-be-headlines. Months later, the ghosts
depart from my wearied sleep. Now it is spring.

Spring is a train fleeing the ghosts' old haunts.
Spring is a glass window shielding me from the projects;
spring is sending the help from a place where money
and music hide the rotting houses and flaking billboards,
while children grasp rusty bikes for dear life as they pedal

across old newspapers – only a paragraph dedicated
to the ghosts. Spring is kids careening over potholes
and broken glass with no helmets, ignoring
the 78 murders so far this year, passing ribbons
of makeshift memorial for the 217 last year
without pausing to look back.

It was May that night & still I wore a wool peacoat[2]

Sometimes when the clouds block the sunrise like it's a burden,
and the rhythms of my day feel like a stainless steel hamster wheel,
I crave the night when we broke into the sandy playground.

My floormates tracked that place's movements for months on end:
frenetic neon-onesied children almost fell over trying to push each other
on too-big tire swings, but at least the tricycles fit their stumps-for-legs.

Their laughter summoned a time when pretending to be an adult
was just a game: cash or credit, let's cover our faces in shaving cream
or put on aprons and make dinner. Hey, look, you're a furry old man!

The navy dark set in when we finally smoked enough blunts
to ignore the dismay of moving out from the building
next to the playground, so we took turns running to leap and grasp

---

[2] Based on Saudade [so-daud]

Portuguese, n.

1. Nostalgic longing for an absent someone or something
2. An emptiness, often with the repressed knowledge that the object of longing will never return, but with the continuing hope that it might
3. In lyric poetry, often carries melancholic overtones and a mystical reverence for nature

the chain link fence and gracelessly flop over, as if we were children
and being a lady didn't matter, and people didn't help each other up
because they were supposed to but because it was kind,

because that's what friends are for. The grit burrowed into my hair
and under my fingernails as we carried a too-big birthday boy
in a wheelbarrow around the swing-set. Next, a plastic yellow house

with a fake fireplace held our crammed bodies. We pretended we weren't
stuck on any sort of life trajectory yet. We held off the good-bye, the abstract,
the fucking big picture, and drank wine like juice. And so the symbolism

at that moment was useless, and the wind numbed our fingers and knotted
our wild mulched hair and dried our skin, but later, on the tire swings, heart beats
rocking gently like a clock, the only sounds I could hear were the synchrony

between the swings and our breathing, a see-saw-creaking. Yet at the pause,
our bodies were still, preserved like we were children playing ghosts in the
graveyard,

paralyzed, frozen and wind-whipped under the stars.

Grady Bennett Myers, Jr.

Mozart

I like to see the dance of the old man's head
The one playing that Mozart impossible
His gray hair ripples like
The dust mop the cleaning woman
Shakes out the back door

Dust particles fall softly
Some blown by the wind
The cello grinds its gritty notes
Like boots dragging
Across a stone floor

Somebody must have shaken Mozart
The boy   right out of him
His father showed him all over Europe
The hurdy-gurdy man with
His monkey on a chain holding out a cup

Kings and counts want music
Who is the great father who shakes
The boy out to make a man
What happens to the dance in the boy?

Perpetuity

The same is always
and the day has been long.
Old men at the seaside.
They come to the boardwalk
and sit on the wooden benches.

They come from far
to spit into the ocean.
No one notices their tiny spit bubbles
nor the men who wear caps with bills

and don't talk.
They are there for days
and no one misses them.

The men who fish
have a purpose.
The men who don't fish
                and don't spit,
                their wives always come to get them.
They will be back next year.
The men who fish never leave.

Ode To Silence

Out of nothing   God
The glory of the nothing
The noise of nothing
When everything goes silent

A blank sheet of paper
Stuck in a type writer
What is the book inside of
Winter silence   the industry
Inside a peach tree
A tree making its rings
A chick growing inside an egg

The night that does not say
The energy it takes to raise the sun
When the wind is not blowing

The man in the moon
A newborn   his only
Speak is the eyes of the look

The noise of quiet   when
The electricity goes off
Listen for the sound of the rock
Hear this poem when it ends.

The Art Opening

Full dress uniform real gold real silk
The woman of means
Handcuffed by her gold bracelets
The heavy metal choker round her neck

Southern woman of means
Real gold
Real silk
Real art.

Standing back I survey the paintings
My thumbs touch the loops holding my belt
An alligator's skin

Alone on the dais
The woman in black….the flautist
Blew out Mussorgsky's
"Pictures At An Exhibition"
While I looked like an art critic
The German art teacher said.

Staring out at the people
Hands on belt
I thought.

What if a slimy alligator came by
To see the pictures
Would he gape and gawk
With his mouth opened as wide

As an accordion extended
And his teeth as sharp as a chain saw?
He'd have a private showing
While the flutist played on.

Jenna Leigh Evans

Absence as Tour Guide

Absence calls attention to itself with a self-importance that doesn't let up, mashing its mouth to the microphone. I'm not permitted to absorb my surroundings on my own terms. Here on Baltic Street I observe the golden gingko leaves frilling against a deep blue sky.

AND YOU ARE NOT TOGETHER TO WATCH AUTUMN DEEPENING, absence insists.

Be present, I urge myself.

YOU MAY NOTICE THAT PRESENCE IS NOW COMPOSED ENTIRELY OF ABSENCE, giggles absence. WOULD YOU LIKE TO PICTURE A FEW EXAMPLES? HER PRETTY HANDS PULLING OPEN A MILKWEED POD, SETTING THE FLOSS AFLOAT?

Everyday Words Seem to Turn into Love Songs

In the aisle of Winn Home & Beauty, it takes under an instant to notice the little pink packet of Beauty Gloves. Under an instant to recog -

(bedside table)

- nize the bubbly illustration of a beatific lady at rest. The thing about an instant is: you can't get in front of it to stop it.

Ha-Ha, Clink-Clink

When you are a child, you are sent to your room while the grownups have their parties. The deep, rich sounds float to you, freighted with pleasure and secrets. Murmur murmur murmur. Ha! Ha! *Clink-clink.*

The story goes: you'll be ready for such fun once you're a certain age. But how is that relevant? Unless you're allowed in to that very party that very second, you'll never know what joke it is that just made everyone roar and clatter their cutlery. No, the child is right: those good times are happening without you.

Mono No Aware

The gingko trees were the last to turn this fall, still flirting with green until the first hard frost, and then all at once, *whap!*

...like a hundred dancing girls in gold kimonos unfurling a hundred thousand gold fans. The sidewalks beneath their trunks are heaped with doubloons. They are given to creating sudden, magical tableaux.

I came upon a parked car they had completely transformed. A drift of leaves had gathered, just so, at the base of the car's windshield, forming a neat yet luxuriant crescent shape. Yet there wasn't one single leaf anywhere else on the car's surface. Spotless and holding its circlet of golden leaves, it looked like a bride on its way to a fairy wedding – this homely, boxy white car.

La Vie En Panic

One thing after another reveals its loveliness to me. Stately old brownstones after an autumn rain have got pendant drops on all their most elegant surfaces: wrought iron that is patchy with rust, sycamore trees wearing waistcoats of English ivy, fancy gourds and pumpkins arranged on stoops, and yellowing bamboo fronds!

These magnificent sights begin to give me the sensation of being a wild animal that has woken up to find itself in a zoo: desperate to locate the home that has vanished and been replaced with something else altogether. I try to reason with myself, but only return to the same crushing facts. *This is really happening.*

Doug Stuber

Pablo and Max

This is the story of Pablo and Max,
They left New York City to avoid income tax
And gather some primitive artifacts.

They left in the rain in spring '52
And were seen in the fields with an African gnu
Admiring the shapes that came into view.

While Pablo was digging up red cube-like art,
Max drew some monsters on government charts.
(They looked like amoebas with elongated parts.)

The days were spent studying carvings of stone,
Or walking in jungles out on their own.
An artist knows how to survive alone.

Always popular with their new friends,
These two went about setting new trends.
They taught the natives how to pretend.

Unlike the scientists who went to steal,
The artists just borrowed that primitive feel.
A congenial arrangement, if not ideal.

The Shining Path

Plant technicians spray
Untold zillions of hanging and or
Boxed flora. Oxygen-producing takes on new
Importance in buildings where windows
Only open text.

That someone might need
Fresh air, never occurred to design
Teams hired to assist architects who sealed us in.
So a whole generation gathers,
Squirts, fertilizes.

Job-production, an
Old game with a new twist, keeps just
Enough folks working to avoid revolution.
The illuminati keep us all
In place 'til needed.

One day the flower
Box jobs may disappear. The meek may
Inherit what is left after the "enlightened"
Have gobbled all the rest. For now:
Dig, spray, replace, dig.

We've woven a web, you and I,
attached to the world, for no matter
how long, inscribed, though poorly, for
scant eyes, still, as bright a love aura as
has ever glowed, tightly wound around
our hearts, yet soaring miles above
Moodung's fog to warm cold February.
Sparks fly off a round-rock fire rarely seen
in these parts. We laugh, it feels like we
shouldn't be here on a cold winter night,
just a few meters from trails so packed
during the day. This charge will never
leave. We've marked this space but must
go to where the stars shine, deer run, art springs.
Keep my heart in your brain, words in your hair.
Matched lifelong yearning bursts in my hand,
fluorescent. Quick, pack what you need, let's
flee! live life in the positive zone, expand
what we enjoy together, bound by the luck
that brought us this far. Where to next?

Play

Brandy barks at swooping swallows,
Life, lowered to one foot or so
In summer time is simple,
As the lure of tired dogs and clover
Greets only those who need to play.

Scampering down outside stairs
Past the skidding bicycle marks
To a tumbling fit of joy
Goes the only daily memory
Of a happiness once known.

Landing in a pile of limbs,
Which includes the golden hair
That shines of wetness on the
Back of Brandy, the player
Laughs at the summer sun.

How long will it be
Before the play begins again,
Before the youthful joy
Once known appears, before
The love, if ever, returns?

Big Bear

We ignored you after 22 – 30 million died
in World War II. Favored China, reliably
corrupt, into having a Feudal class, but you lacked
the prowess to extract your own oil, we could still
do oil business with you, Big Bear, but the rest
went to China: the shipping, manufacturing, even
new mergers wherein Chinese firms now own Volvo
and the PC division of IBM! So Sochi was to be
Putin's horse, so someone burned Kiev right then!
(CIA?) Distressed, due to the viciousness of events
around the globe, neighborhood, we divert attention
from our own digression at home to a potential
(yet again) war in a third party's country, Ukraine,
which NATO is willing to exterminate in order to lure
today's tanks into a larger skirmish in case the ISIS

crisis flames out. Gotta have back up wars and back
them up in case the main wars sputter. It's a new
Pentagon directive, as witnessed by the annual troop
and ship movements every March on the North/South
Korean border. Tom "Obama-Hawk" drones fly again.

Kingsmen

That day when Di and Dodi died apocolypse prayers
were read. Not in hopes that it would never come true
but in the belief that population control is best observed
from safe castles in Scotland while the religious split
deepens via CNN, Fox, fundamentalists all: each mosque
now jihadist, each church raising coffers, a la Falwell, for
the CIA, large jets, troop and arms logistics, as a large
multi-theater war persists with nary a peep of descent.
A small yellow desert-flower, maybe five inches high, with a
half-inch diametered blossom shakes in the wind caused by
seventeen tanks rolling by. A hand shoots up, it's a 14-year-
old girl volunteering to blow up a cafe, and herself. The
beautiful, quiet, consistent hum of a drone belies its
mission: to bomb the house of a suspected terrorist.
Parchment, hand-made when the artist pulls soggy fiber
up through water, accepts ink that seals the fate of grunts,
jarheads, bell-bottoms, and flyboys who have already been
in harm's way for 13 years now. We're approaching Crusade-level
madness, yet the protests, if any, don't get covered: TV war scenes
staged to replicate PC-Games as kiddie-propaganda becomes reality.

Jaki Shelton Green

buried kinships
a poem for Shelby Stephenson

how long does it take
to name everything
you've ever known and loved
July, a slave girl
a tonic of wisteria
black-widow web
she is the book
we are lifting together
from a communal shelf
of washed southern ground
she is the book
we read together
potion for forgiveness
pouring from the tips
of her fingers
july
the early morning lesson
for all our sons.

Stillbirth

my plants thrive whether i water them or not in this house museum of tragedies smudged handwriting that does not translate into any language smeared across walls crawling out of equatorial fog mass a bloom of tropical air lifts your hair into this dry horizontal wind inside this house a wind you deny we love beneath bedraggled backyard roses they too hold shadows sadness in their petals a slap of razor to the walls whispering morning sorrow becoming song for the death of things green the eroticism of suede bare sleek wood glass balls hanging steel bulbs is not lost on me i awaken in the center of the slave girl's dream not that one but this new slave girl in the center of her winter flower dream in the center of white clustered petals inside dark praying palms fingerprints pressing hard against make believe wedding dress a bouquet of nettle primrose queen anne's lace her life barely a whisper barely a whimper from the floorboards of an open book her heart remembers all the flavors of danger she married them all before in another dream beneath canopies of thistle lace spread over burial grounds singing wisteria one legged sparrow dagger -toothed womb sassafras mouth she married them all in geeche swamps moss covered lynching trees houses built on rooster bones liquor stills cotton plants that cry when you touch them my heart opens in the center of the new slave girl's dream where her vows are a shudder of blessed death stronger than any other light she swallowed before stronger than this dream dust i birthed you in april you were nobody's apology nobody's unadorned table you made the dying worth living i am the scribe paid in silver a shepherd girl barely old enough to tell her story she opens my hands and counts the silence the emptiness inside each space of joint that is dead breathless I know my hands have emptied many wombs cried for the remembrance of dead babies lost shepherd girls my hands now receive all the disguises of everything i have forgotten how to name how to count how to love.

the seasons within

i

like the resurrection of dry sticks
stems struggling for rebirth
a crying in their roots
the replanting of my gardenias
i too cry out
in my bones
in my veins
small waters break
travel through me
slippery like morning dew
reminding me of dew
kissing my grandmother's garden
a garden always in transition
perennial and annual all at once
marigolds calendula lilacs
hydrangea lantana zinnia
butterfly weed
as vexing as verbena
as punctual as petunias phlox wisteria
as elusive as magenta tulip magnolia
as evasive as vintage peonies
whose health mirrors my own

ii

i come silently to this healing place
revisit my own birthing
the birthing of my babies
like the ancestral gatherers
before me
i come bringing my health

i am reminded that i am a late-flowering verbena

the doctor is my age
i have prayed for a doctor
who is also a gardener
it is there in her hands
telling her story
hands like my hands
tawny gold shades
that speak of autumn pruning
seasonal lathering with eucalyptus lemon balm

i am reminded that i am a late flowering verbena

when she points her instrument of light
to the back of my pupils
she recognizes the night-blooming cereus of my childhood
she is not astonished
that her lab tubes
soak up chlorophyll from bloodless veins
i allow her to strip this bark
check the tree of me
that is flowering
the roots of me
that leave a trail of descent

iii

we dance the dance
of patient doctor
friend sister
woman child
the scent between us
is honeysuckle elusive
ancient patient
the scent between us
is ripe health
the smell of morning rising from the earth
scents bring memories

birth death
light dark
the doctor listens for the faint rustle
within my blossoms
soon there will be
a silhouette
in my rooting bowl

i am reminded that i am a late-flowering verbena

iv

only a gardener
would leave seeds scattered
across such barren ground
only a mother
would watch the sun
measure the rain
caress hold roots in place
like the fruit bearing trees
that came before me
i too wait
praying for rain
holding onto the hands
that guide direct gather
my healing

all verbena has a season

a litany for the possessed

cultural whoremongers
appear on MTV
disguised dapper fresh
as third day bleached linens
from a sun not raised
on cotton indigo or gold
shaking singing ringing
baking dipping gliding
stomping sliding prancing
bebopping dancing praising
hip-hopping slipping slurping
belching fucking

grave pirates
sucking on the bones
of spirit prophets
malcolm ray miles
martin charlie
eldridge audre denmark
sojourner frederick countee
nat langston zora
louie richard nell
mahalia billie bessie
marcus gwendolyn
kwame toussaint mohammad

kente tie-dyed
refried batiked bleached
mudclothed dreaded blonded
matted twisted reddened
curled permed blackened greened

slinging
swords of quran bible torah
bringing
lies death deceit disgrace
juneteenth blood bones
sipping on holy water
that runs backwards

cultural whoremongers
holding hostage
prayers altars crosses
allah-hu akbar
axe
amen
namaste
shalom

addicts with poems
stuck between their teeth
join the night
pray for a vampirical moon
bootleg poems
sold beside remixed coltrane
rinsed out aretha sonnets

poets posing as undertakers
slip nip tuck drain
splinter irrigate protract
stitch catheterize graft
skin to word skin to history
skin to lies skin to truth
skin to battlefields in algiers
iraq vietnam korea somalia
johannesburg selma brooklyn
compton queens atlanta richmond
detroit afganistan

poets posing as seamstresses
sew faces sew teeth sew wombs
sew laughter sew tears sew regret
sew joy sew uprising sew anthems
sew constitutions sew treaties sew bombs
sew graves sew babies

brothas on the down low
sniffing for game
while sistas play
diva bohemian princess
sable goddess queen mother
high priestess of counterfeit
on a corner

that becomes continent
sahara amazon latin kurdish

the new immigrants
learn to walk
talk
become invisible
eat fire
twist glass

flat joins round
night forgets that
day is his true sister
rivers forget to open to skies
freedom is exposed raw naked
unadorned unnamed

cultural whoremongers
dressed up as words
metaphors preludes
benedictions
die alone
under skies that rant
retrace the scorn
theft murder
lynching of
a fallen muse

humble light
for Imani

the full hand lifts
from an empty basket
children happy
***
skirts raised
a full moon roars
the daughter eats stars
***
spring snow
in the empty house
the woman child kisses her own hands
***

brown hands coiled
inside white arms
the one less afraid
lifts the curtains
***
we watch the stars together
purple lace fancy shoes
race through puddles
hold our tongues still for raindrops
for a purification of the heart
***
late may
the family waits
summer friends feed them
early june
winter friends return
***
above the wailing
a dragonfly soars
thirsting for tears
***
in eastern sky
rainbows cast shadows
the granite sky leans
***
i'd like to kiss seeds
in this quiet place
sprout grace
***
beyond the river
ancestral crones clench their palms tight
stitch prayers in the hair of newborns
***
the breath remembers
***
light rain
kind women listen
hear the whisper
repair the fractured wing
***
in the new place
early morning dew
the coolness of many hands
***
the seagull sits alone

listening to the sisters sing
a mother watching from a closed window
***
two dragonflies dance
towards the open window
the daughter closes her eyes forever
***
flash of sky
grandmothers remember
other nights of blooming petals
***
night strolling requires more
mother of pearl shoe buckles
gardenias bird of paradise primrose
wind in hair feathers blue opals
borrowed dreams
from the medicine woman
***
the boat is not sinking
a thousand hands braid the waves
offer ransomed wings
***
blue night nymphs
rehearse morning dance
over and over again
weeping hands cup knead fold trace
face stomach breasts hair legs hands
still-born opera
***
your sister places a single white lily
across your heart
i should have told you more stories
your great aunt lily
taught me to see in the dark
***
suspended tears
shrouding of light
your morning of storm
visitation of angels
dark men bearing glass gloves
***
friends help me lift the boat
in the middle of this ocean
i don the glass gloves
friends return home

plant basil blueberry trees
bake bread write poems
listen for sirens
***
in the kitchen
i am never alone
ginger garlic collard greens
eggplants chocolates
pots baskets spoons bowls
sing stories of other seasons
***
in the church
chandeliers sway
a thousand tiny lights
lifting the fallen dragonfly
from my lap
***
the wings bear crimson
a homage towards evening sky
remembering other flights
***
whisper whisper my lovely
blue black green dragonflies
dust themselves
in amber lavender frankincense smoke
seven angels weep
swallow the dragonflies
incarnate veiled watery azure
organza womb breasts hands lips

Frank Doonan

August One Park

August One Park, early spring.
Couples waltzing to Titanic.
Scrape pickers pass, brassy ring

Ocher and sienna, red tide passing
Desperately seeking roots
Sprouts return, roots deepen

Birdmen, cages in neat rows
Fans wave, drums roll
Bird dance in shadows

Erhu and Opera, scraggly pine
Hawkers layout assorted morass
Carved stone, bits of shell and rind

Freshly made brass and glass
Gray sunrise, goldfish and art
Passing pigeon, hopeful glance

Hiding from passers by
Pale green jade, blush of silk
reveals itself to the patient eye

Eyes follow, no one says hello
Gossip and vain hopes occupy minds
Chinese calligraphy, old snow, yellow

Faint aroma, dumping in the dark
Plastic bags dancing in wind
Flap of a worn deck, foolish carp

Players curse date of birth
Next deal, a better hand
Tai chi flows gently over the earth

Clueless hope picks a stick
Worn can of old man

Fate weaves a web, careless pick

Vain hope, a new name
When the fool leaves the park
Little red book reads the same

Noon, leave the dream of maybe
Return to the marked deck.
Tomorrow, again pretend to be free.

野有死麇 yě yǒu sǐ jūn: A doe is slain

A poem written likely as a protest to male violence against women.

野有死麇，白茅包之。 yě yǒu sǐ jūn, bái máo bāo zhī.	A doe is slain, In white grass wrapped.
有女怀春，吉士诱之。 yǒu nǚ huái chūn, jí shì yòu zhī,	A maid longs for love, By the hunter tempted,
林有樕朴，野有死鹿。 lín yǒu pǔ sù, yě yǒu sǐ lù.	He hews the forest, Another doe is slain.
白茅纯束，有女如玉。 bái máo cún shù, yǒu nǚ rú yù.	In white grass adorned A maid pure and soft like jade,
舒而脱脱兮，无感我帨兮， shū ěr tuōtuō xī, wú yǔn wǒ shuì xī,	Approach gently and softly, The waist cloth untouched.
无使尨也吠。 wú shǐ méng yè fèi.	Be gentle and not aggressive. My dog protects me and barks.

竹竿 – **Bamboo Pole** (59), 衛風 – The Odes of Wei

A daughter of the House of Wei is married in another state. She expresses her longing for her home and the pleasant life of her youth she describes in the poem. She was probably the Baroness Mu of Xu. From the 《詩經，诗经》**shījīng – Book of Poetry**

竹竿
藋藋竹竿、以釣于淇。
豈不爾思、遠莫致之。
泉源在左、淇水在右。
女子有行、遠兄弟父母。
淇水在右、泉源在左。
巧笑之**瑳**、**佩玉之儺**。
淇水滺滺、檜楫松舟。
駕言出遊、以寫我憂。

Bamboo Pole

Bamboo pole, to fish the Qi.
Should I not consider
. . . these gentle thoughts of far away.

Crystal Spring on the left, Qi River on the right.
A woman desires to be with
. . . her brothers and parents far away.

Qi River on the right, crystal spring on the left.
Longing for the soft smiles, and healing jade pendants sway.

Qi River bring me joy, juniper oars and pine boat.
steer my thoughts on the journey
. . . to home far away.

木瓜mù guā, **Quince.** . From the 《詩經, 诗经》**shījīng – Book of Poetry**

投我以木瓜 She tossed me a quince
tóu wǒ yǐ mù guā
报之以琼琚 I gave her a carnelian rose
bào zhī yǐ qíong jū
匪报也 Not in gratitude

fěi bào yě
永以为好也 But to forever reminisce
yǒng yǐ wéi hǎo yě

投我以木桃 She tossed me a peach
tóu wǒ yǐ mù táo
报之以琼瑶 I gave her carnelian, wine red.
bào zhī yǐ qíong yáo
匪报也 Not to be grateful,
fěi bào yě
永以为好也 but a token of love remembered.
yǒng yǐ wéi hǎo yě

投我以木李 She tossed me a plum.
tóu wǒ yǐ mù lǐ
报之以琼玖 I gave her brilliant black stone.
bào zhī yǐ qíong jǐu
匪报也 Not to repay the sum,
fěi bào yě
永以为好也 but to never be alone.
yǒng yǐ wéi hǎo yě

芃蘭 pénlán: **Sparrow's Ladle** The Sparrow's Ladle is a Milkweed species that has pods shaped like the prong, a claw or canine tooth-shaped pendant, 佩觿 pèixī. The leaves of the Sparrow's Ladle are often curled into a shape resembling the 韘shè, the archer's thumb ring. This poem has distinct sarcastic tone about the overstatement of the claims of men during courtship. The prong is worn by men when they come of marriageable age. The archer's thumb ring is a symbol of status and achievement of the skills of archery. The 佩韘pèishè is an ornate pendent carved in the style of the archer's thumb ring. It's worn as a pendent and not on the thumb. Using a reference to a pendent instead of a thumb ring may be an added touch of sarcasm, because the archer's thumb ring pendent is too ornate to be useful as a thumb ring. These articles will be made of fine jade, jade-like stone, ivory or bone depending on the status of the person in society. . From the **《詩經, 诗经》shījīng – Book of Poetry**

芃蘭之支， The Sparrow's Ladle is propped up
[by a stick],

péng lán zhī zhī,
童子佩觿。
tóng zǐ pèixī。
雖則佩觿,
suī zé pèixī,
能不我知。
néng bù wŏ zhī。
容兮遂兮,
róng xī suí xī,
垂带悸兮。
chuí dài jì xī。

The lad wears a fine prong.
Despite this handsome prong,
He cannot know me.
He desires to statisfy,
But his girdle swings low.

芄蘭之葉,
péng lán zhī yè‘
童子佩韘。
tóng zǐ pèishè。
雖則佩韘,
suī zé pèishè,
能不我甲。
néng bù wŏ jiă,
容兮遂兮,
róng xī suí xī,
垂带悸兮。
chuí dài jì xī。

Like the Sparrow Ladle’s leaf,
The boy wear’s the archer’s thumb ring.
Thou it is just a pendent thumb ring,
He cannot protect me.
He claims to fulfill me,
But his girdle hangs low.

Renata Lader

Predawn Path

The beers last night
won't let me sleep longer,
a soft toilet seat finds my butt.

A half glass of water quiets thirst,
sweat socks on my feet
lead me to the sleeping patio.

Two silhouettes follow them meowing,
dry cat food misses bowls,
rolls on floor creaking under my steps.

An empty bladder sends me back
to flannel sheets where my husband's
warm body swallows me.

Thanksgiving Day has begun.

Father on the Wall

I watch her climb up on the couch, stretch her hand
and with the softness of a two-year-old,
she touches the cold, shiny paper. Her daddy
smiles to her from an enlarged picture displayed
on the living room wall.

Her eyes, blue like Forget-me-not flower in the
coloring book she will give him the next,
half-hour-visit in prison, look up at the picture.

She moves her fingers over his hair,
stops on the forehead, gently caresses his cheeks.
She gazes into his dark eyes then whispers,
"I miss you daddy, come back, I'm a good girl."

I clench my teeth, tears on my cheeks.
How can she comprehend her daddy's passion
for truth against a communist government

that left her joined to loneliness
and mama's sad face?

Storm

Gusty wind forces grass to kneel.
Pregnant drop of rain,
the single tear
of a coming monster,
splatters on a dusty stone.

Anguished skies lash
with tons of rain, water rages
in a newly formed trench.
Thunder, like low-toned trumpet,
announces imminent dread,
your voided affection.

Lightning ricochets, parts demonic
blackness, like an eagle
with its yellow beak, thrusts a fierce
arrow at the bowing pine tree.

A fiery aura of sparks
illumines lightning-charred trophy,
greedy flames lick the trunk, black
smoke spews departing breaths.

Satiated, the storm
gathers its weapons, thunder
murmurs on far horizon.
I am hollow.

Memorial Day Celebration

Goose bumps on my arms,
tears on my cheeks. I listen
to a famous singer in a sparkling dress,
her patriotic songs rise to the gray skies.
An enormous American flag flutters.

Thirteen years in Iraq and Afghanistan,
thousands dying – the ultimate sacrifice, they say.
Their souls departed, indeed free.
The surviving invalids angry, suicidal, bearing
survivor guilt – the ultimate sacrifice
of distorted minds and spirits.
"Pray for a miracle because you'll need it,"
the words of a commander don't mean much.

Year after year, after year,
uniformed officers stand at the doors of over 6,800 homes,
"I regret to inform you …"
The families left with this earthly life,
nights of shrunken hearts, clenched teeth,
their days lack a purpose.

On a screen in front of honored guests and the public,
video clips of hide-yourself-and-seek-the-enemy,
explosions in rough terrain, uplifting speeches,
mentioning World Wars I and II, dramatizations,
as if the real drama isn't enough,
the overly theatrical voice of the narrator
make my fingernails dig in the couch's cushion.
I yell "Shut up! Shut up!"

I do honor those fallen, I do respect those living
with their missing-body-parts, I send prayers to their families.
Still, my question stands: Why do we, the people,
let disastrous wars control us?
Why can't we learn not to fight?

Edward Lyons

In Golden September

Little butterfly
Drying your wings in the sunbeams
Hush, little girl
Hush –
Listen, let me give you a gift
Made of all I have suffered,
All I have learned in this world
In this life.
Take all
Understand all
Know that it was all for you.
And then, little butterfly,
Fly with your own wings
Fly toward the infinite blue
And let me return to the twilight
Where I can see you
In the night
Where we can go
As we were when we lived in the middle
Of the city
And you were a beautiful girl
And I was a man
In golden September.

Below the Springs on the Rainbow River

Nighttime mist, drifting off the
water, has filled the
whole air. Young people from the suburbs,
tired and amazed how last

evening such love, such love of
being, being Here
could have flowed like candlelight, their melded voice
around the four guitarists,

now, like awakening birds,
salute the day. She
stirs the ashes; he lays needles
and twigs on the dim coals,

and the breakfast fire kindles.
Unfocused strummings
Invade the shattering mist. In twos and threes,
They wander toward the table.

Ode on Solitude

I

The fell season has laid dark branches bare,
And faded dim sweet memories of summer
Like sunset sapped by cruel boreal air,
Until I feel it's ever been November.
Brittle sheets of ice float on pools
Among withered cattails rimmed with frost,
And overhead sail flocks of flying geese,
And meadow flowers fall like broken jewels,
No more to feed the laughing dizzy bees,
For joy, like teeming summer, has been lost.

II

Like a song out of tune I wander alone
In darkness of Orion and his foes,
Whose starlight glistens on the casement stone

Of dreary mental fortress built of woes.
No woman's blissful touch eases my breast;
No woman's eyes peer into my own;
My lips taste no woman's warming kiss;
No kinsman stares with me into the west;
No singer comforts me with magic tone;
Nowhere my weary soul find peace.

III

No doting friend can peer into my thought
Which meanders like the restless stream
In whirling eddys that cannot be caught,
As I pursue in vain a fading dream
Of roses blooming on a summer lawn,
And splashing love beside the happy sea,
And notes plucked sweetly from an old guitar.
The few contented hours I've known are gone,
As now from halls of light I wander far,
Cast out, condemned, weeping, yet wild and free.

IV

Freedom treads on beds of fallen leaves
To gaze through tangled boughs on wintry sky,
And drink deep silence when the cold world grieves
Where lines of marble stones in churchyards lie.
I roam such landscapes in my vagrant mind,
As honest men feed warmly at their hearth,
Lost and lonely, lashed by biting wind,
A wan ghost sailing bleak and wasted earth,
Searching sadly for what I'll never find:
The rainbow's end, and songs in flowery birth.

Dry Season

The sun blasts the sky to seething white.
At this height of summer, the air is a kiln

That bakes the corn to stalks of clay.
The river shrivels to mud beneath the railroad trestle.

Through the haze, a row of trees across the pasture

Looks like a ridge across a valley in dead winter.

The grass burnt to dust around the
Wooden idols that decay at haphazard angles.

We've always counted on these to bring
The bit of rain that kept the land alive.

Locusts hum in the stillness of afternoon.
Silently we watch the land wither.

Around bonfires the druids chanted desperate litanies,
Making burnt offerings of our sleekest cattle, our fattest sheep,

Until the smoke of brushfires has risen across the land.
Still our livestock grow thin, our horses weak,

And still the idols rot in the desecrated field.
Come winter, nobody will stop the poor families

Who live down the road from bringing their
Rusty rattling trucks to haul them off for fuel.

We didn't notice that first breath of wind tingling
The chimes, but now it blows the hair back from our sweating brows,

And we look to the east where great cumulus clouds
Loom so bright in the late sun they make us squint.

They come nearer, rumbling, flaming so bright
They seem like envoys of some living god

A god living in the grass, a God whose breathing
Will restore our corn and make our herds grow fat.

Surely the clouds will come and bring the rain.
The cool falling running swelling miracle of rain

Must come, as surely as the setting sun
Shines golden on the backs of horses.

The Wild Rose

Those were better days.
The rose bloomed on a wild hilltop
Near where the town's main street became a country road.
In those days, hikers climbing there
Smelled the musk of its blood-red flowers,
And painters came to paint
The points of sunlight playing on its leaves.

On a warm afternoon in August,
The townspeople gathered at the foot of the hill.
A band played songs they all knew by heart,
On the grass they ate sandwiches & drank beer from bottles,
On the grass their children played tug-of-war and blind man's bluff.
That evening when lovers walked quietly away to the rose on the hilltop
And others walked home,
They all thought the vague sadness they felt
Was from being tired out after a long day in the sun.

In the middle of the night,
Something went wrong. By morning
Banners lined the streets, and posters
Of a shadowy enemy with fixed bayonet covered
The walls of the public buildings.
Soon conscripts bivouacked on the hill
Saw the rose's dun and brittle leaves drop,
And women from the brothels saw its blossoms blacken.

It is late November.
Jagged clouds cover the sky. They will snow.
The geese have gone far south.
The rose's thorns lie snarled on the hillside
Like barbed wire across battlefields.
The wind drones like a sullen motor.
A pale red glowing glows in the east.
In the bitter cold of winter,
The bombers will come, and after them, the big guns.

Elegy for All Souls

1.

In dawn's grey light,
Hope of sleeping fades
On dreams hurled into daylight
And the time of the laughing water is never,
And the acolyte's step on the rainbow staircase is never,
And any love youth valued once is over,
When the sun shines under half-drawn shades.
And when I understand
That to reverse the tide of waking is to reverse
The world that turns the sun's course,
I concede a perhaps more pleasant realm
To the tyranny of time,
And accustom myself to being awake.

2.

And how can I speed the six hundred minutes?
How can I overthrow the tedium
Of the clock that enforces the unvarying
Non-negotiable exile?
And can I perhaps regain
Something of the freedom
That dawn abolishes?

3.

Question the reality of a field at nightfall:
See grey swirling vapors

I call clouds, darkening clouds, and below
A billowing line of black,

Trees, which I know by day must have color,
(and what if some morning wind rustled blue

Leaves beneath a yellow sky?)
And that slick angle must be the road.

And into what wooded hills does it lead?

Surely there must be avenues

Like where the girl who was my friend
Stood beneath a lighted neon sign,

And the hard light of the telephone booth,
The shine of headlights beyond, halogen dawn,

And the station wagon passes. And what
Does it pass? And what does it not?

It has not gone by her sexual fantasies,
Or yours, or mine, nor by

Victorian novels,
The New York Stock Exchange,

Nor the Bible,
The laws of Newtonian Physics,

The legal courts, dialectical
Materialism, nor perhaps even spirit,

But it passes a tree that whispers in the rain,
A miracle, tower of tumbledown leaves,

The shivery surface of a waterfall
That passes, like the girl who was my friend

Through memory, and into the imagination.
And now the evening is an enormous

Toccata and fugue played on the motion
Of sun and planets

And the convergence of windbelts
That bundles and binds the stormclouds.

4.

In summer, at sunset, the colored sky
Made galaxies of gaps between the leaves
Of the woods outside.
I remember midnight dew

On the velvet grass far away,
The telescope I craned my neck to see through,
The hazy orange halo
Of the nebula in Hercules.
It was like the flaming ball I followed beyond time
Through the piney forest on the ridge
That shut out the evening sun,
Over the summit, into night.
From a high ledge I saw the lights of the city.

5.

In a night hour I stepped
Through a hallway, the air
Saturated with smoky diamond light,

Heard music, Haydn, heightening
Through twists and stairwells
Until I came to a double door.

The crack between beckoned,
And I looked through it to another
Atmosphere, a vision, a shadow

Of an angel sat upon a stage
With violin tucked under chin
In waves, haloes of yellow heat.

6.

I have a stone mansion:
On the grand piano stands the fat bronze horse,
I have carven furniture, Chinese figurines, Apollo's bust in marble
A porch of flagstones over the demesne
To the high tree where I caught my foot
Trying for a bird's nest.
There are huge canvases, showing forms and shades of color, energy.
My house is haunted, they say.
Once, coming from the peacock roost, I heard a ghost
In the kitchen, rattling glasses.
I keep expecting I'll see it gliding down the stairs,
Or find a gallant party whirling in the parlor.
The starlings caw in the morning,

And the mighty spirits who dwell upon the walls
Keep me awake at night.

7.

Washed by hot yellow waves,
I took the road through the blue forest,
Winding through the hills that rose
Into mountains, through mining
Towns, along the grass
Of river bottoms.
The peacock cawed upon the tower of grey
Boulders, standing on the moss
Before the silver spillway of the waterfall.
And if you can discern,
Survey the mental landscape into cities and counties,
You will find what your skill is worth
After you sojourn beneath streetlights, an meet
The ghostly girl who was my friend
Forlorn in the light of a laundromat,
Or at the pay phone without a dime,
And give her coffee and sweetbun.
And then if you still would know divinity,
Disbelieve all your thoughts;
Undertake the realm of silence.

8.

Has this vision a thousand facets?
The pollen grain
comes to rest on the anther,

The candle

burns on the alter,
The mottled leaf loosens

from the twig and flutters
the river mud fans beyond the

delta.

Look ardently:

four mountain ranges on the walls
sing silent music.

In the brightest green,
fingers of rain ring
the surface of the lake,

A breeze plucks unseen harpstrings,
the billowing run of notes
is a firework of flowers.

The green deepened in yellower sun,
from the nearby smoke
comes the call of the starling,

And a distant flash,
tenpins, or the roll
of kettle drums, thunder.

A grey swirling sky,
windwhisper of orange and yellow,
tâches detachment, flutterdown the breeze,

Fallen, shifting, gathering like dunes,
and they rustle and crunch
as a deer springs over.

Driven by a terrible wind,
snow howls over boulders,
a dissonant symphony,

And the sun rises low and icy red,
granting the stark peaks and glacier,
a blue stillness.

9.

A new wind invades
The heat of a strange blue forest
From a cool distance,
A vanguard of autumn.

A spray of raindrops falls
From a galloping thunderhead
Patters on the tall oak's leaves,
Roll downward leaf by leaf

And the arc of their falling
Connects the fire ends of branches,
The turning dry begins at the top,
Spreads downward

Until only the grass below is wet.
Look carefully with your glass:
Each leaf is speckled
With minute brown flaws.

The wind will bring crimson, gold,
The unspeakable beauty
Of a boulevard on a wet night,
Bronze lamplight melts into the pavement,

Torchlight in a royal armory
Blazing on shields and bullion,
Red drops on the windshield, headlights
And the runny lake of green.

The whirlwind, scuffling dead leaves
On macadam, opens the fissures of memory
A procession of moments and people I once knew
Wells into my brain and blows by.

Ahead, beneath
The rain-drenched oak,
The girl
Who was my friend

Holly Holt

"Woodland Wanderers"

We, woodland wanderers,
crunch leaves underfoot
while a black dog, panting,
errs in believing that we
know the path back home.

Small stream, rock-strewn,
formed from autumn's tears
chutes down the foothill.
"Follow it!" you declare.
"It will lead us back home."

The haunt of memories
aches my yawning soul,
recalling a jaunty trek,
autumn's play of light,
and home's safe certainty.

"Just Then"

Where did my mind wander, just then,
chasing a blue jay's flight? Work,
the cry of home-bound labor, stifles
whatever lethargy hides within—
for movement is the call of hours,
attention is the seconds of striving
forget-me-nots, surmounting a hillside,
weary from the weight of a vast bower
beyond the rise of busied, dense days.
Where did my mind wander, just then,
lost in the details of a quiet Sunday?
... and is the blue jay as jaded as me
by the thought of what must be done?

"how dust settles"

isn't it strange
how dust settles
on bookcases and desks
like seeds of promise,
aching for denouement?

how sad, that Unknown
where heathen gods
refuse us the grace to remember
that not everything
will be read,
or written,

the floors won't miss
our footsteps, pacing
or our golden dreams
pirouetting on velvet afternoons
with friends, family,
or in fevered solitary
where genius thrives

all we have
in the end
is dust
on bookcases
desks

& ourselves

"Observing Time"

every day
a part of us
observes time

you say
i'm depressed
and drunk

if i'm depressed,
let it be

within the raging core
of my heart

to soften me
to console me
to guide me
to squelch my fury

for time and I
both know
i'm not meant
to last long

i'm a tender-hearted,
foolish girl
broken by thoughts
better left alone

remember this
when i'm no longer here

and that i was drunk
on borrowed time

"Georgia"

Candles come, go,
in this fickle weave—
fireflies' full failure
to highlight pages
of Southern scripture;

dirt road hiccups
in rocks and puddles
that radiate with rain
(summer in transit);

roadside roses blush
beneath green boughs
dappled in honeysuckle;

in all this stillness,
moon's bashful glance

over mountains high
whispers in pale light:

You are grace,
sweet Georgia.

Joseph Milford

70.

i only knew you as the boy who got lynched but was
good at math and your ghost was geometry.
the tree branches all hung with tethers which changed
history& the trees were ashamed for us.
now golf-cart trails wind through woods as leaves fall.
werewolves working the shopping malls.
flint, ash, sycamore, thistle, bear-oil, hickory, locust,
cane staff. the tendons and sinews respected.
its November. St. Hubert and the deer rut. he cured rabies,
brought the hunt to the church masses.
twelve-pointer striding up to us with rosaries
and crucifixes in its antlers. killed it immediately.
your eco-poetry hieroglyphically spreading like
moss and lichen over the downtown buildings.
let pregnant women put rusty nails in the garden
to ensure the bountiful harvest. moon waxing.
hung the empty hornet's nest in the kitchen for luck.
still were divorced. you re-married a wasp.
divorce means "to turn away"—as if walking out
of Hades after looking back. as in salt pillared.

71.

the Geiger counter goes clickety when you walk past
the tent. we are coccyx deep in this project.
under the word CROATOAN was inscribed R'lyeh
in Palmetto treetrunk. foolish hick teenagers.
you tickle a baby's feet it will develop a stutter.
they cut the wings off Thelma's twisted ankles.
your hippocampus was named after a seahorse.
olfaction of fresh conch. limbic sense of tides.
the verandas collapse into effluvium. the gardens
splendor into conflagoration. no vendettas.
i was no Lapis Exilis. i just fell off the porch. full
of ham and wine and whiskey. the fool again.
yet rising up just fine like the morning star to secure
the rigging at the mooring of beginnings.
carving the sphinx in a bar of soap. carving the face
of Alexander in an apple. it leathers well.
hummingbirds dueling with the dragonflies
in the pagoda-light of the edenyard now bronzen.
deer being the moon herds being the Bacchic being
the steeds of light being sustenance and arc.

72.

empanadas. funnel cake. cotton candy. deep-fried
Snickers bars. diabetes with wings circling.
pingpong ball. fishbowl. catapults. balloon and darts.
crossbow shoot. everything is rigged.
funhouse here from the kitchen to the bedroom.
distortion in your hall-of-mirrors eyes. schism.
fanning the bonfire with a plastic dustpan roasting
marshmallows on chicken bones. family.
everytime i listened to you snore in the recliner
next to me with your Maker's Mark and oranges.
you were an authority on petroglyphs but couldn't
change a diaper. derelict at church functions.
fishing wire taught around the garden hung
with strategic Xmas ornaments. deer eat good here.
funhouse here from the bathroom to the back porch.
you glaring and gleaming. my no remorse.
it's a $50,000 fine for hurting an amber snail.
thus, Montezuma's treasure won't be unearthed.

& i have other get-out-of-matrimony schemes.
lottery tickets. maps. robberies. forgeries. cons.

73.

Papa Joe said it's cheaper to keep her. he says women
sleep with who they want. men with who
they can. he says spoon her at least three times a week
or someone else will keep the bed warm.
he says show me a beautiful woman and i'll show you
a man who's sick of her shit. he was
married for 54 years. after Marvene died, he followed
a few months later. all i ever wanted to inherit
was his boxes of arrowheads. he had taxidermied birds
lying all over the house. a cuckoo clock in the dining room.
old piano covered in church hymnals. the carpenter's workshop
where he would make us wooden swords and shields
and hatchets. many foxes grow grey but few
grow good said Benjamin Franklin. Papa Joe said
man has his will but a woman has her way.
never marry a beautiful woman if you want to
sleep at night. these old school buzzards, you got to
love them. the World War II men who raised us.
the World War II women who reared us.

74.

banana spiders creeping about the front steps
and beer cans behind hedge. grass needs cutting.
nights all like waiting in emergency room lobbies.
in between tests. blood pressure off the charts.
Stretch Armstrong crucified to the live oak tree
always disturbed me. neighbors' kids possessed.
hipster rich pseudo-lesbian sitcom babbles inane
while preparing bowls of lemons and beersalt.
she said I watch *Forensic Files* to know how to get
away with her murder. sip my beer quietly.
it's good luck for a virgin to piss on the fishing nets.
we couldn't find one in ten counties. Cajuns.
once i knew i couldn't study at Crotona with Pythagoras
i dropped out of Bowdon High School.

explains everything really. reading *Prince Namor* comics
at Red's barbershop as men lamented.
banana spiders by back porch where the stray minx
birthed her mangy kittens. feral green eyes.
question was not why couldn't you love one another.
that's a stupid question. grow up already.

75.

wandering sojourner stray mutt lab-mix saunters
by drugstore panting or smiling with purpose.
life is confessing adultery to a priest who is now
fucking your wife. abdomen full of buckshot.
a group of rhinocerouses is called a crash.
pahoehoe is smooth lava. i want to crash you on fire.
you won't buy antiques because they might have
a demon yet you refuse to exorcise your own.
Tuscan, Doric, Ionic, Corinthian, Composite.
Solomonic is particularly difficult. adult education.
your words and wounds daily crocheted into a cap
for the newborn. you don't find this creepy?
you aren't Catherine of Aragorn. i will not behead anyone.
still, i could cut out that liar's tongue.
i tried to get you to read Ron Silliman. i tried to
read Ron Silliman to you. Ron Silliman on Mars.
now stray is climbing into the concrete culvert
after something; he's whimpering. maybe rabid.
i didn't learn circular breathing for you.
i didn't grow extra fingers and hands for you. megalo.

Jasmine Farrell

Jazzy

My voice and its chill tone
is my silhouette.
You can't forget
me once I speak; you can't help but
become intrigued
by the lil lady
in Chuck Taylors
who named the pair Marie.
My lil switch doesn't declare
I'm in the room.
You're too swooned
by my smile.
Sucked in by my big heart
and kind words.
My genuine intentions
speak before I even part my lips.
No need to be tipped off
about what I stand for.
My motives are more transparent
than the core of a wine glass.
I just want to encourage, enlighten, and challenge the
malevolent to seek a safe resolve...
Intently involved with my own convictions
in addition, to seeking what breaks God's heart.
I'm a part of a clique that holds no
qualifications.
Just warriors who fought
diverse situations that should have executed
the sparkle in their eyes.
I don't demand the spotlight.
The world assumes I want it.
I'm just confident even in my flaws.
Why not flaunt them?
Why not let them know I hurt like *she* does
and get angry like *he* does?
Why not let them know that I believe in God for what He is now and was?
        Sovereign.
Why not proclaim that we should all be in this together,
using my lil ole poems?

Why not show them there is no need to belittle another being
who bleeds the same deep blood red?
I just want to encourage, uplift and find beauty in
the cracks that were once closed.
I suppose heads held high are intimidating to heads hung low.
Nobody ever likes anyone so free and open with themselves.
That's why I'm so compelled to go against the grain
while, learning to love the fibers that are pulling on
the masterpiece I'm trying to create.
I'm aspiring to just be...

Neon Hints and Bold Signs

I embodied our yesterdays like
vintage prose in anthologies.
Probably since apologies are never
in order for our skeletons.
I stood between your wounds
and
the softest part of your essence.
        I understand...
You couldn't see the authenticity
in my switch,
couldn't catch the hints in my quintessence.
It was evident to the world
I just wanted your core.
But, you craved more hints
to hush your irrational fears.
I embodied every part of you
like cocoons to caterpillars.
Did you at least consider the motions
my heart was making?
I watched your walls slowly disintegrate
and rebuild once I saw
the raw parts of your presence.
        I get it...
You couldn't discern my yearning
to embrace the dark corners of you
too.
You couldn't see my neon actions
that spoke, "I love you."

You're A Star

You're a star, but you're too scared to shine.
So, you dim your glow to
blend in with the midnight sky.
Love,
the world needs your light.
It's looking for your bright
ambiance that tickles
the sternest minds.
Shattered hearts are wishing upon
you, even though they can't
even see you.
Your core is the truth,
enticing deceit to alter its motives.
I suppose your wounds were intended
to stifle your growth.
Don't be afraid of **beautiful**.
Don't fear your shine.
Step over the line they told you
to never cross, Love.
You'll see how the points made you what
you are-
for the better....

Better Without You

You made it crystal clear.
Nevertheless,
my eyes simulated your *authenticity*,
even though
your heart revealed atrocities
more wicked than Pol Pot's philosophies.
I was blinded.
Intentionally threw my heart in a blood red sea, hoping
it was sweet tropic blue.
I front like I didn't give you vulnerable parts of my mind.
Like I'm not scared that letting you go would put me in a bind.
Like I wasn't inclined to receive your
rapacious ways.
Like I wasn't receptive to the new you, despite its poisonous attributes.
I would love to say that I am not in love with you.
I want to declare that I'm better without you.

But, I can't seem to believe such a veracious utterance.
There's so much substance in, "I'm better without you."
So much love for myself in, "I'm better without you."
I don't need your help in, "I'm better without you."
I will no longer be put on your shelf in, "I'm better without you."
At least I found my worth yet again.
Following the hard to gulp down truth of your shady,
180° degree
transitions.
At least I walked away with tears flowing, dignity still whole
and empty hands.
I still don't understand what happened.
Occasionally haunted with *what if* thoughts and silent replies.
I want to declare that I'm better without you.
I ***need*** to declare that I'm better without you.
But, I can't seem to believe such a veracious utterance.
There's so much substance in, "I'm better without you."
So much love for my own self in, "I'm better without you."
I don't need your help in, "I'm better without you."
I will no longer be put on your shelf in, "I'm better without you."
Oh, I will someday.
With my hands on my hips and my heart guarded on a
steel pedestal
Once the fool, I'll wisely declare that I'm better without you.
For now, I'll drape my emotions with strength and

heal with the support of loved ones.
Funny, I thought you would be one of them.

Preston Martin

Abiding Image of Rome

How poor I would have been
if I hadn't heard and seen
your Vespa screech to a stop
as I stood lost, on the curb.

A vision in that exhaustive haze,
in that instant you became
the embodiment of precious recklessness,
that handful of days,
the bloom of seventeen-or-so
                                        and endless summer

          washed in ancient light,
          eyes searching, impatient
          with an idle pace, you teased
          the throttle and charged your throaty Vespa
          through the writhing knots of cars
          clogging the piazza.

I am far from there
yet you come to me more and more.
My mind peers into your quick eyes,
I hear the rattle of the scooter
and watch your soft silhouette
disappear amid the ruins.

Promise

There is nothing sweeter than that first crack of thunder,
the sweep of purpling clouds over the crowns
of trees, buffets of wind, the clatter as whirligigs
spin and sing. Birds flutter and chatter,
soar and dive on the flux of the moment.
Fat air parts the grass weaving a path
across the yard, around and through the startled pines-
over our neat lawns and ordered lives.

These past days, temperate and level,
morning to night in calm proportion. Now
billows of wind and drumming rain offer up
a grand commotion, whisk the muddy musk of earth
with the scent of splintered lightning, that wet electric
fragrance of storm that cheers my expectant heart.

Summer

She led Granddad down the yard
to his chair in the shade. His straw hat pulled low,
to his dark glasses, his checkered sweater loose
around him against the shadow's chill.
Soon he asked Grandma to take him inside
the tool shed. She placed his good hand
on the doorframe of the two hole outhouse
dug in the corner of the little building. She waited
outside for his call and led him away.
Then I slipped in.

Inside was dusky and smelled
of dirt floor, must, the tang of kerosene. Odd
shapes were tarped in the shadows. I ran my fingers
over worn handles and pimpled steel of hoes and saws
hung on the rough walls. Light shot through the cracks
and strung golden threads about my head.
The air percolated,
particles swirled and looped in space.
So happy.
I grew dizzy with the mingling scents
of moist earth and piss and shit, the circling
of motes and light.

Kitty Bergel

Beginnings, Again

Yesterday, it looked like a tiny spike winding out of leaves
today it's a small new leaf, burgeoning.
                How?
An hour ago, the earth's core
released tongues of aa lava atop the island
and now there's new land, steaming and night black,
Auguring well:
                Earth beginning once more.
A whisper starts a breeze, and soon
gale force winds tear at the trees:
                Take cover and pray.
A zygote, predictor of a human
being, divides and forms into a fetus that
will suck its thumb inside the womb:
                Comfort is welcome at the beginning,
                the end and in between.

Beginnings, propelled by forces
a scientist only begins to explain, are
ferocious and slight, tender and mighty--
all around you, all the time beginnings, and
their partner, deaths.

The first beginning was like the split-open
Egg, broken by a birdman in Rapa Nui eons ago.
It was the Word.
It was the land forced to open
by a coyote spirit in the long ago midnight.

The second beginning is in more human terms.
It requires silence, listening,
trying to know, courage, and the right time.
It builds upon failure and folly.
Appropriating strength and perseverance
of mighty trees and remembering what you
can't forget, what you won't claim, what
you don't want---calls forth mists of
primordial places where first movements
began, where first winds blew,
where waters coalesced and deserts

rose from depths. Beginning again is like
the first beginning, only you are wiser,
freer, older, closer to death and closer to
the next beginning.

A thrush still sings,
a small resilient hope.
Where are you, what is the hour?
What do you desire,
What do you love?

A Memling Madonna

Ave Maria, all hail!
In the folds of your blue robe
There is room enough
To gather our sins.
Your flaxen hair is for
birds to nest in.
Your downcast eyes
Absorb all our sorrows
With sweet serenity.

Ave Maria, how will it be
When you no longer sit in glory?
When the Crusaders set out
on their death marches,
When the Inquisitors lustily scourge
When Joan of Arc is burned alive
When the death of God is proclaimed?
Hail Mary, full of Grace:
What will happen to me?

Creating the Universe

In the eighteenth century,
far away, an Easter Islander
painted pigment,
possibly blood, on stone. Look:
the image of the creator god Make,
a Birdman
holding the broken egg
from which the universe

was hatched.
How was it to create
the image of the creator?
some cultures
forbid this,
some laugh at it.

How did Make come by
that original egg?
was he pleased or did he
bellow with frustration?

Did he know that most
of his creatures,
parts of the universe,
would die in war,
would die of pestilence,
foolish ambition?

It's more than a single egg
that made the universe.
It takes love beyond life,
hard labor, deep feeling,
sorrow without remedy,
wondrous beauty, far-reaching music,
delicate moist places, searing fire,
mountainous cataclysms,
schisms that come together,
changed forever,
and fissures dividing for all time.

No creator is
big enough for
the night sky that
neither begins nor ends.
It takes the death of
each of us,
the birth of our children and theirs,
countless animals, sun,
air, water, plants,
endless time,

imagination and grace.

For Sleep

Around midnight I turn off the light
reach for sleep, and hope
that it won't take long now
and that I'll dream well.
I don't turn to either side, I
relax my head, wanting
ease and quick slumber before
the worry clock begins.
I'll not try, I've done sufficient of that today.
There's nothing to mollify, nor any
beauty to admire. Enough has
happened for one day.

Morpheus wafts out of starry clouds,
slides around and perches on a cumulus
poof, while angels trumpet dulcet chords from the corners
of the realm. Zephyrus, off to the west,
puffs out his cheeks and sends sweet breezes
trailing down through the universe;
faintly glowing stars barely pulse
responding to the desire of the Milky Way
to encircle the known sky. Tonight is soft velvet, sleep
comes, and gentle rest.

Slowly, slowly.

Madonna of Rocamadour

A Black Virgin, dark now
due to age, but quietly regal:
of black walnut wood
dried out over long years, she now
seems smeared—anointed-- with ash.
Jesus, a small man, perches
upon her knee, inclines into the world,
no longer part of his mother.
Her face is worn, her eyes
blank, unseeing,
unjoined from the world.
her calm is everlasting,
as is her sorrow.

Ave Maria, *grazia plena*:
you are an effigy,
small and angular, imperfect:
who has absorbed
the world's grief, sadness
and betrayal.
You have sat on that throne
for untold hundreds of years;
your emaciated arms barely
hold you upright
The jeweled crown,
added recently,
is incongruous, yet majestic.

Oh dark Queen of heaven,
black queen of earth,
how do you bear
all these pilgrims' hopes and fears
secrets, desires, disappointments,
along with your own foreboding?
What upholds you
knowing what you know?

Let me join you
I will finish living
then die into eternal time.
You, you wait for the least of us
with dark hope.

Ramon Ramirez

Winter Man

The winded willow wails
a crescendo
hovers
where wild flowers grow
in the giant's shadow
way below
weathered leaves
whisper,
creep through the shed door
that yawns
each time Winter Man raises his axe:
blade-on-bark
creates the sensation of 'being there',
and a wry smile — thin,
like dawn's frosted moustache
over the Chevy's windshield —
transforms his black lips
into worn wiper blades
that stifle the sound of his teeth
chipping away
at Winter's breath.

Polaroid Blues

Standing by the window, Polaroid in hand, the man stared out at the hubcap rolling in the sand. Now the screen door, she was whistlin' a sad and lonely tune; and the bastard dogs outside started howlin' at the moon.

Midnight clouds roared and the sky came apart at the seams. The man tipped his cowboy hat, looked up and saw where Jesus hides his dreams; they glittered gold, blinked purple-pink, and he was sure the little girl in the picture winked.

A crackle and hiss as Sun's fingers scraped over the curtains;
here and there bookshelf dust sighed — of this he was certain.
Feet up on the whiskey-stained table,
he smiled back at the four week old mud grins
on the toes of his boots.

A snap of his fingers and the Zippo lighter flamed to life —
he lit a cheroot, watching as the smoke draped his fingers,
watching the cat on the window sill
curl itself into a ball, stealing
all of morning's secrets.

A black house spider crawled over the rip in his jeans;
the man jerked his knee back, and tilted his felt cap —
each word he spoke was covered in smoke
as he welcomed the *little fella*,
and cursed the world outside.

Amanda Gordon

Into The Darkness

Into the darkness.
An unknown realm.
Stepping unaware.
Deeply cold.
Hollowed Silence.
An eerie steel.
I am alone.
Falling through.
The darkness promises nothing.
For no option near nay there.
A simple blackening.
Of my air.
The darkness consumes me.
Leaves me breathing heavily.
The distant sounds.
Creates a Lulled barrier.
I am the darkness.
A deep wound.
A scar to carry.
Forever subdued.

Anxiety

Sometimes I find myself.
Teetering on the balance.
A cryptic world.
Full of doubts.
Encapsulated by pain.
I'm simply bleeding.
Stricken within.
A heart of steel.
Can't differentiate.
What I'm supposed to do.
An agony so bright.
Turmoil proceeds.
Sometimes slipping.
Losing grip.

Drowning.
Swallowing.
What's left of my air.
Beaten and undone.
Completely Stunned.
Combating the darkness.
Simply on my own.

Moonlit Snow

And then the moon came up.
Within the silence.
A blizzard flows.
Howling winds.
Emitting.
A fury blow.
Footsteps treading.
Within the snow.
Misted darkness of a calming realm.
Into the white.
Paths obstructed.
Distance unknown.
Blurry vision.
Countless drops of frozen flakes.
Remarkable light as evening wakes.
The promise of night.
Beginning to settle.
Peeking through horizons.
Shining uncontrollable.
Subtle hints of colors.
Within natures palate.
A world's lullaby.
Beginning night's transition.
Droopy minds.
Resting souls.
Beautiful images.
Of moonlights glow.

Paul Aaron

You Are a Song

Elaine, the mother of Sir Galahad
a torch, the light, brightness

Easy now to say you are a song
(a long forgotten melody I've found again at last).
Let sing, and only then secure some sense.
And then the melody will bring us more.
I sing to share our harmonies and see.
Now riffs can soar to say that
Even we must sing to know for sure.

Vines full of song we shape to sing of notes that form.
I search the soul to satisfy.
Now is the someone that I say can solely fill the hole.
Search for the notes that make the sounds that save the day.
Oh sense God's song to show that
No one else can help attain what I desire.

More. Thank the source of
All that is.
Right makes us sing.
Yes sing.

Elaine's bright light
Can make it easy.

Do sing.
Rehearse.
Enunciate.
Whip out the words or never know the song.

After the storm

It was a quiet storm
on a quiet North Carolina February day.
Saura, your eyes opened widely.

Our curtains shivered in the spirited wind.

Out the window flew my soul
with yours as
rain fell hard
from my eyelids.
It was all over
so suddenly.

It was then the tree limbs fell around us.
Earth split open its craggy domain.
Rocks falling, as from the sky
meant nothing to me
but a cover for your grave.

And there was nothing.
Birds and buzz saws were silent.
Car engines faded off into the distance.
A last whistle sounded from the train.
You will be with us no more.

The breasts that I loved to touch
are cold now,
a last lingering kiss on cold lips,
no longer a lover's thrill,
but "good-bye."

We do not need to fight
with the wind and the rain.
Nature's bigger moment
has come upon us.

After the storm is over
there is a quiet blue
in the silent sky.

I Heard the Imam Say

I heard the Imam say, “The jihad, the holy war, is the fight in my own heart. I walk with compassion to all hearts.”[1]

I heard the Rabbi say, “When I step with loving-kindness, I cannot step with the harsh boots of war. When I strive, it is with the angel on the ladder to heaven.”

I heard the Buddhist Monk say, “My words are like jewels. They travel thousands of miles. My actions are the ground that I stand on.”[11]

I heard the Pastor say, “God tendeth my flocks. One day my lamb and lion shall lie down in peace together.”

I heard the author say, “He looked… into the heart of an enemy and saw there love and understanding. Wonder came into his face… he smiled.” [111]

I heard Sensei, “In Aikido, there is no enemy. I draw in those who confront me; tumbling with me, body, mind and heart.”

In the Library, I heard the Atheist say, ”I forgive the truly evil. I stand strong in my belief that I not miss the mark.”

I heard the Priest say, “…the flood to wash away my sins… the fire of love to make me pure…zero population growth to create world peace.”

I heard my heart say, “Help me purge hate; find peace in this heart. Hear, my people, the one who created us is one, and all of us are one."

Pogo said, "Beware the enemy for he is us. [1111]”

[1] From the words of various Imams after 9/11.
[11] Based on the words of Thicht Naht Hahn
[111] J.R.R.Tolkien, The Lord of the Rings, the elvin queen, Galadriel, and the dwarf, Gloin
[1111] Walt Kelly, Pogo

Butterflies, A Few Years Ago

A few years ago I was walking in Duke Forest
When I saw a hundred large, black butterflies
Covered with spots of color
Dancing in the air over the ground.
They rose about a yard high, then descended,
Lit again on the ground and circulated back up
Like sparks in a small, hot campfire.
I watched for a long time, then
Saw they flew above an object on the ground.
Curious, I slowly made my way over
To see what it was.
I didn't want to disturb the butterflies,
But did.
I was twenty feet away
When they sensed my movement.
I thought I was quiet, almost still.
They soon were gone, and all that was left
Was the object on the ground.
I walked over to see
It was the droppings from some large dog,
A bear, an errant human, who knows.

Some of us are bears,
Some of us butterflies.
I pretend I know my way around this earth,
Stomping where I want to,
Scaring off butterflies.
I think there's something wrong with people
Who can't face up to my bravado.

My daughter scares off with the quietest approach.
In these last few years, I've softened.
I still scare her off, thinking I'm speaking of something helpful.

I think I'm the wise owl,
Speaking little and saying something wise.

The owl is a predator.
It tears the living daylights out of its prey,
Leaves little for pretty butterflies
To eat.

Murry Handler

And There Is Quiet In The Sound Of Air

I have reached
A very high
Altitude in age
And can see a far distance
From my mountaintop.

The air is good
And the view clear.
I am looking for God,
But cannot find Him.

My assumption
That God is a man
Should be obvious.

If God were a woman
Would She allow
The children of Africa
To starve?
Or Indian girl babies
To be cast aside at birth?

Screams from women
Being raped around the world
Would surely reach her ears.

Bombs tearing flesh
From bone:

In Palestine,
In Israel,
In Afghanistan,
In Sudan,
In Congo,
In Iraq,
In Colombia,
In America,

In Russia,
In Chechnia,

Would touch Her.

Millions of Jews
And Tutsis
And gypsies,
Might have lived
Peaceful lives.

She wouldn't know
about religion,
Only Goodness
Only love.

She wouldn't care
About names like
Jesus
Jahwa
Mohamad
Allah
Only goodness
Only love

She would be wary of
Permeating greed
Angry fundamentalism
Compassionate conservatism
And neo anything
Only goodness
Only love

Some people
Say they have found Him
But it hasn't changed
For the world because
No one believes
Anyone else
Finding God Is real.

I have reached
A very high
Altitude in age

And can see a far distance
From my mountaintop.

I see tall
Mist covered mountains
Lakes and streams
Of blue velvet
Ageless, twisted
Wind formed trees
Rock formations of
Magnificent proportions
And there is quiet
In the sound of air

And I am waiting

Meg Wethington

Fall In

midwinter gunmetal
sharkskin waves
gnash and clash
thundering tempests roll in sets
ring in quaking earthen chests
pulsing
against my mother wit
and the beach

Hera's chambers
colliding fighting shifting rising
leap
for the flaccid arms of Zeus
the billowing smoky heavens rise
drag sagacious feet
turns his lofty back

the ravenous seagulls and i scream
stand outstretched
against the argentine sky
on the edge of the Nun
methril laden armies of clouds
gather sift slather mound
against the incensed fires
riding against the ashen sea

the ground
the sand
the beach
terra firma
hard beneath
Gehenna's speech loud

my breath
my voice
delivered out of reach

beside myself i stand

sitting on the edge of the eastern continental shelf

watching
waiting
for breaking bits of light to begin
fighting for freedom
stiff thumb punch
though the cardboard night
the sun bellows
in the shallows beneath them
sticky shadows drown
and there's
no place to hide from forgiveness

Day Seven

sunshine finally stung my
skin today
as i gathered my breath
and the limbs from the ground
that were scattered
carelessly during
winter's war
spiked pinecone grenades glow amber
matted spring mess
weighed wet and heavy
on the battlefield

Tease

Flirting with the fingertips
          of half-naked limbs
chocolate brown leaves
     flutter
        and
                fli p
                     flickering
                    and   flashing
           their   backsides
taunting golden yellow promise.

They wave-
laughing at me
in their
freedom
fueling the fire of the
daily desire to
break away
and join them-
and burst like a
spiraling summer bu b b le
sparkling iridescent
into the warm sunny surprise
of a sapphire sky that
lays outside
my spider's
waxing winter window.

Visit

i watch the
shapes of them
glide past
feel collective eyes
so near they're here
beckoning beneath the water
with the twinkling twilight
barefoot standing on sandy beach
i walk towards the
shifting silhouettes
just off the banks of
my mind's shore
and i
collect heavy curiosity
in our bones
my legs get wet
in attempt to
walk out to meet the
mystery of knowing you
and freeze frames my mind
i'm floundered i apologize
the whole too big to see inside
i try
i don't get close enough

steady breaths go
knock-kneed under
their gazes in awe
the liquid living light
between us conveys
betrayed by sad long knowing
we ache

Jazz

caught between
the smooth flat curve of trombone tongue
and the embouchure of crooning clarinets
hair messed in a jazzman's broken sigh
alto sax scaling up hot thighs
feeling the rhythm- sworn
to a jazz flute's secret trill
finger zingers demand
deep long winded notes
chasing shrinking hemlines
changing faster than the beat
short skirted staccatos kick up ivory tickled heels
and squeal in the syncopated rhythm
quick spank of skin on a conga drum
tilts a high hat shady to a
sultry trumpet begging
to be in that number
proverbially hard pressing
questioning the silence's addiction
to return to itself

jazz

Richard Smyth

BOOT POEMS

Old Boot

I will go with the boot
into distances
the long haul through life

The boot will be with me
in summer mud,
on mountain trail,
through winter mist.

It will hold me
like a mother holds her child
and I will be warm and safe.

The boot will never wonder
of arrival,
for it knows the worth of journeys.

There is never a need to ask
what the boot knows.
It speaks in footprints,
summits, departures:

the rapture of passage,
the humility of mission.

New Boot

Shining soldier,
bright with polish
and tight as forced smiles

you come to me
the way newborns come,
screaming for love.

I will offer myself

humbly
as any sacrificial flesh.

Over time,
we will begin to see
the meaning of horizons.

Boot: Anthropomorphized

There are some simple decisions to make:
are the eyes on the outside
or on the inside?
How thick is the skin?
[no stanza break]

What kind of strings are attached?
How tight are the stitches,
how sturdy the soul?

Such accidents will determine
the way it walks through the world,
the way it holds the memory of mud.

Boot: Broken

You will be broken
like a horse,
bent to my will,
you will wrap yourself around me
the way space parts at my passage,
washes over me like water,
you will become a means of leaving,
a kind of striding off into the sunset.

You will be giving like a mother
or a loving wife.

You will lift me over mountains
and, no doubt, when the time comes,
we will walk right into heaven
as if no great distance

were traversed.

Boot: Triumphant

The boot will bear the weight
of many sorrows.
It is strong, it is
made for this,
this living on,
this pulling through the mud:
ox in its yoke,
kite on a string
wing in the sky

The boot knows the mud
for what it is:
something that holds one back,
something that swallows the weak.

There is always mud
on the way up the mountain.

But the boot holds me tight,
carries me like a child
toward the summit
where the view will be
[no stanza break]

breath-taking
breath-giving.

Boot: Theomorphic

The boot will bear me
towards heaven
through the gates of hell
and all its psychic fury
up the rungs of the body
through the spaces of the brain,
synaptic distances.

I let it take me
where it will:
I had no idea
the road to heaven
led through the body.

Boot: Metaphysical

Not the boot
but the idea of Boot:
concept
essence
abstraction
extradimensional in the
Always Beyond
where All Things are capitalized
to signify their pre-existence,
their perfection:

It is here
in the mind of God
that the Boot began its journey
its long walk through time
to arrive in my life
right when I came to the foot
of the Mountain.

Boot: Miraculous

We speak of the miracles of modern science:
laser surgery,
quantum computing,
ten-dimensional superstrings,
but we sometimes forget
the simple miracles of the mundane.

Take the boot, for instance:
flesh of destinations,
[no stanza break]

host of horizons,

it sacrifices itself for us--
not for our sins
but for our ascent.

We must remember that,
in the time before wings,
the boot was our one tool
of transcendence, a technology
of vision.

So let us praise the boot
and all that it offers us:
the journey,
a way through the mud,
a virgin birth of becoming.

Boot: Deified

You can read of how natural
this process is
in the journals of neurotheology:
the deification of cognition,
the assumption of wonder:
miraculous
radical.

And so it is with the boot:
once we recognize its role
in our lives--
the way it separates us
from the animal earth,
the lizard instincts,
and lifts us towards the heavens--

we will build it a temple,
fall upon the altar,
spill ourselves in sacrifice,
sing hymns in praise
and give glory
to boot.

Boot: Petite

Petite *boot*
--not petite bourgeoisie:
as in booties,
small soft things
for small soft feet.

The petite boot is made
to prepare the young for the world:
[no stanza break]

for a lifetime of cover-up,
hiding, protection:

soon there will be alarm bells,
gated walls, barbed wire
around the perimeter of our homes--
to keep out the shoeless ones.

Boot: Inhabited

Sometimes the boot is big enough
to house whole families

as in the Old Woman
who once lived in a shoe
and was evicted for failure
to pay rent
so she moves in to an abandoned boot.

This is fantasy after all:
people don't live in boots, shoes,
unless there be giants,
drunk, stumbling shoeless
through the moonless night.

Boot: Strap

It is thin leather
looping to the top of the boot:
something to hold onto
after you've fallen
and you're trying to get up.
The only thing to hold onto
according to those who know
human nature: cowboy philosophers
carrying guns and Gideon's.

So when you're down in the dust,
remember that the boot
is not just for the foot
but is a hand, immanent
like a prayer, thick
like skin.

Boot: Camp

This is no summer camp:
no fun here no tether-ball
no crafts or competitions
of the civilian sort,
but a place to learn
[no stanza break]

the arts of war.

This is where boys become men,
learn to tie their boots,
long tall black leather,
new soles thick for the long march
home from hell.

Boot: Sculpture

The boot in this sculpture
is not large and soft
or cast in bronze
or on some overlarge hero
of a war memorial.

This work is conceptual in nature.
It is political in content.
It is a sign of those
who died in Iraq,
a war to secure our standard of living,
despite what the soundbites say.

There is a pair of boots
for each soldier killed to date.
They are lined up as if soldiers at roll call.
They stand at attention,
most drooping like dead flowers.

Just a regular boot.
One that you or I might wear.

Steve Bloom

Appetites

You cannot stop smoking
   although you know it is killing your lungs.
You cannot stop eating
   although you know it is killing your heart.
You cannot stop producing and purchasing useless junk
   although you know it is killing your planet.

Something profoundly human in this,
   I guess. Still,
it does seem like a shame.

Allow me, then, a small proposal:
Forget all of the international conferences
to negotiate treaties that probably won't work
and that no one will observe anyway, even
if a treaty is signed which it probably won't be.

Let us call one, final and definitive
international conference
to rename the earth "Easter Planet"—
after that Pacific isle,
once an abundant paradise,
over-indulged to the point
   of starvation.

Visit there today.
   Take a voyage into your future.

The massive monuments
we have constructed
will remain standing too,
   for a time.

And aliens who come down
to visit a few centuries from now
will, perhaps, after a quick
assessment, place a small plaque
   before they depart:

"Something profoundly human

in this," the words will read. *"Still,
it does seem like a shame."*

City Life

When the water puddles
on the concrete, filling up
your sewers, you turn an umbrella
to the sky in self defense, discuss
endlessly—with anyone who
is willing to listen—how bad
            the weather is
                        today.

When the water soaks into the earth,
filling up streams and lakes,
the Lakota mother, living
on her sacred land, turns her face
to the sky, smiles at the rain
which brings water—the source
of all life—blessing her,
            her children,
                        all of their relations.

I cannot say that this difference
answers each and every one
of the questions you
have been asking yourself
about what is wrong with your life.

But it might be someplace
for you to begin your search.

How to get Rich

I have it figured out.

I will create a genetically modified
sunset, patent it, then make sure
it's the only one in the sky, so
every time you and your lover
hold hands watching as

the western glow hovers
just this side of the horizon
I can charge a users fee.

I did think I might simply
write a book titled "How to get Rich"
and sell it on the internet.
But this idea is better.

"How about writing a poem
titled 'How to get Rich'
and selling it on the internet?"
You ask.

Forget about it.
I will never get rich
by writing a poem.

Valentine's Day

It takes a great poet
to compose a great love poem.

But even the writer of mediocre verse
can have a great love.

Bargain

I walk by the store-front gym,
have to turn off my hearing aids
to keep from being blasted
off the sidewalk by the music
pouring out through the open door.

Lots of people inside working up a sweat.

There ought to be a sign out front
I think to myself:
"Build your body
Destroy your hearing
All for one low price"

Sounds like a bargain.

Mini-Biographies

Phil Morse is the author or co-author of five books, including *Does a Pigeon Bark?: 212 Fun, Educational Activities for Young Children* (Anteater Books, 2009); *Gloria Mae, the Heroine of Dunkirk Harbor* (Anteater Books, 2009); *Face to Face: Communication and Conflict Resolution in the Schools* (Sage/Corwin Press, 1996); *Young Children at Home and in School* (Allyn and Bacon, 1995); and *Home-Style Learning: Activities for Young Children and their Parents* (Prentice-Hall, 1981). An award-winning poet, Dr. Morse has published in *The Poets' Corner, Selected Poems* (Intercare 21st Publishing, 2006); *The Journey* (The Links, National Resource Center, Spring, 2006); *Sand, Sea, & Sail, Night Whispers, Exit 109* (Old Mountain Press, 2007);and *Bay Leaves* (North Carolina Poetry Council, 2007). In 2007, he received an honorable mention in the North Carolina Poetry Council Contest for his poem "My Son Wishing Me Goodbye."

Pam Baggett's work appears in journals and anthologies, including The Atlanta Review, Crab Orchard Review, Kakalak, Kentucky Review, San Pedro River Review, Forgetting Home: Poems About Alzheimers, The Southern Poetry Anthology Volume VII: North Carolina, and Creatures of Habitat. A freelance writer, she's the author/photographer of the garden book ¡Tropicalismo!.

JS Absher co-hosts readings at Flyleaf Books in Chapel Hill, NC. His poems have appeared in two collections (*Night Weather,* Cynosura, 2010; *Burial of Anyce Shepherd,* Main Street Rag, 2006) and in other publications, including Southern Poetry Anthology: North Carolina.

Asha Gowan is 20 years old and hails from Carrboro, North Carolina. She is currently attending UNC-Asheville for her Bachelor's in Literature with a Creative Writing concentration. Recently inducted into the Southern Collective Experience, she's currently crafting an epic for publication and writing a novel over the long-term.

Dr. Vivekanand Jha is a translator, editor and award winning poet. He is the author of five books of poetry. He has also authored one critical book on the poetry of Jayanta Mahapatra and edited nine critical anthologies on Indian English Writing. His works have been published in more than 100 magazines round the world. He is the founder and chief editor of two literary journals, VerbalArt & Phenomenal Literature. Websites: www.vivekanandjha.com; www.verbalart.in; www.phenomenalliterature.com; Blog: http://www.poetvjha.wordpress.com; https://en.wikipedia.org/wiki/Vivekanand_Jha; Email id: jha.vivekanand7@gmail.com

Deborah Hall: If someone were to ask me, "are you a poet, a singer, a writer?" all I would say is, " I sing in the shower." There is a voice that calls to those of us who must create to protect our underbellies from the surgical knife of life, this is me. My credits for this armor and sword are my three children, my grandchildren, my lovers and the pain that I carry within my body every day. These are the stories that compel me to write. These are my credits and to them I owe my voice.

Robert Okaji earned an undergraduate degree in history. His April 2015 chapbook, If Your Matter Could Reform, is Dink Press's initial offering in its National Poetry Month series. Publications include Boston Review, Clade Song, Otoliths and Vayavya, among others. Additional work may also be found on his website, at http://robertokaji.com/.

Dianne Decaire: "The shapes and colors of the poems emerge as abstruse clues. They crystallize in a way that surprises even myself. I like that surprise. At some point an exclamation [!] of blizzard sharp awareness occurs. Better than a piece of cake."

Angelaurelio Soldi hails from Cremona, Italy. A retired Physics professor, he eases just as often as he complicates his life by painting, writing poems, feeding birds, watching trees grow and thoughts roam on farmland.

Yeon-seong Park is an instructor at Chonnam National University, Korea and is also a poet/researcher. She has published several books including *W. H. Auden*(co-authored with Bom, Dae-Soon, 2005), *Creative English Practice* (2009) and *Dances with Anticipating Ants* (2010). She resides in Gwangju, Korea with her husband who has love for music and history.

Arnold Johanson is a retired philosophy professor from Minnesota who retired to Durham, NC in 1999 and started writing poetry. His poems have appeared in numerous journals and anthologies, and he has published three chapbooks, the most recent *A Trunkload of Ephemera,* forthcoming from Finishing Line Press.

Ruth Carlin, a native New Yorker, singer/songwriter, cabaret performer, and mother, has written poems since the age of fifteen. She is thrilled to be making her publication debut.

Bruce Lader is the Director of Bridges Tutoring, an organization that educates multicultural students. His poems have appeared in The Bloomsbury Anthology of Contemporary Jewish American Poetry, Blue Earth Review, Poetry, Talking River, Confrontation, Harpur Palate, New Millennium Writings, and many other magazines. His most recent book is Fugitive Hope from Červená Barva Press. Discovering Mortality (March Street Press) was a finalist for the 2006 Brockman-Campbell Book Award. Nominated for a 2015 Pushcart Prize, he won the 2010 Left Coast Eisteddfod Poetry Competition, and has received a writer-in-residence fellowship from The Wurlitzer Foundation. www.brucelader.com.

Priscilla McCelvey is an EFL teacher and a poet. She graduated from Colby College in 2013, where she majored in psychology and also studied human development and creative writing. There, she studied poetry under Adrian Blevins. This is her first publication. Her email is plmccelvey@gmail.com.

Bennett Myers, Tar Heel born, an English major at UNC but did not write until the nineties prompted by Coleman Barks and the Men's Movement. He lived years in New Hampshire and writes about granite and the rocky coast of Maine, nature, and his Southern heritage and Grandpa poems. He credits the Friday Noon Poets of Chapel Hill more fertile to his writing than reading from the classic poets

Jenna Leigh Evans's recent publications include *Prosperity,* a Novel, The Nervous Breakdown, The Toast, Autostraddle and the Billfold; she also reviews fiction for Electric Literature. She's a LAMBDA Literary fellow and a Barbara Deming Memorial grantee. Find Evans's work, and her author-interview series, at jennaleighevans.com.

Doug Stuber, recently returned from seven years at Chonnam National University as a visiting assistant professor: he plays ball with James H., paints with Kwang Suk Park, leads memoir writing classes at homeless shelters, and supports budding artists of all kinds. He has published 12 volumes of poetry and in numerous journals. dougstuber@gmail.com; dougstuber.wordpress.com

Jaki Shelton Green, Publications (Carolina Wren Press) Dead on Arrival, Dead on Arrival and New Poems, Conjure Blues, singing a tree into dance, breath of the song, (Jacar Press) Feeding the Light. 2014 North Carolina Literary Hall of Fame inductee.

Frank Doonan is 68, and a Baha'i and poet living in Hillsborough, North Carolina studying, writing and translating poetry related to Chinese culture and Celtic Irish poetry. I lived in China from 1999 to 2006 studying Chinese, Culture and Translating Chinese poetry and references to Jade Culture of China. I also wrote poetry on contemporary China. I also write poetry in the Celtic and Irish styles. In 2007 I started the Orange Dog Poetry Society of Hillsborough, NC.

Renata Lader's artistic talents include photography, painting, jewelry-making, pine-needle basketry, quilling and quilting. She has published poems in The Village Rambler, The Final Draft, and The Sounds of Poets Cooking anthology. Originally from Poland, Renata is a member of NC Poetry Society, living in Raleigh, NC with her husband and two cats. She is completing a memoir about experiences during Communism and the Solidarity workers' movement in Poland, and a book of poems about her perception of American lifestyles during her house-cleaning services. www.RenataUniqueGifts.etsy.com

Edward Lyons has written poetry for 35 years on diverse subjects. He strives to give the reader a window on the transcendent. He is living in Winston-Salem, N.C. where he has joined the city's ancient Moravian community, which is the subject of his current work.

Since August of 2013, H. Holt has been published by various magazines and blogs. She has recently been accepted by Negative Capability Press, who will be including her in their Anthology of Georgia Poetry in 2015. She lives in the luscious mountains of North Georgia, where she spends her time helping students achieve their dreams of higher education. hollyreneeholt@yahoo.com

Joseph V. Milford is a Georgia poet. His first book of poems, *Cracked Altimeter,* was published by BlazeVox Press in 2010. He is currently composing his epic, Tattered Scrolls and Postulates, which will contain several volumes of 10-line deconstructed sonnets.

Jasmine Farrell is an author, poet and freelance blogger. She is from Brooklyn, NY and has a Bachelor's degree in Communications. Poetry is her niche and internal rhyming is her favorite poetic device.

Preston Martin is a retired teacher who continues to teach and tutor, and to study and write in the Chapel Hill/ Durham area. He has poems in literary journals, a poetry festival chapbook and an anthology.

Kitty Bergel, transplanted to North Carolina from southern California, has written poems off and on for many years. She enjoys Friday Noon Poets in Chapel Hill and local poetry readings. She resides in a retirement community, reads a lot, paints and writes. cbergel@nc.rr.com

Ramón Ramirez is the author of Bangkok Street Dogs and The Mighty Mekong Blues. He lives in a small village in northeastern Thailand where he rides his tractor and writes poems and stories (sometimes at the same time).

Amanda Gordon (Rareity) prolific writer, author, poet, and musician.
"I believe it is our mere essence to believe we can achieve."
Musician-hood is my birthright
Writing is my soul.
Together they're my calling.
A beautiful story told.

My previous publications include: "Storied Wheels" A SOMOS PUBLICATION (a short story) Title "When I Was a Little Girl" Page 153.
Rareity.wordpress.com; rareity@yahoo.com

Dr. Paul Aaron's publications include: *Our Blessed Love Enduring* and *Catastrophizing,* performed by Deep Dish Theater Company. He practices Chiropractic and Acupuncture, offers a self-hypnotic/Meditative countdown; helps bring you to your deep core intuitive knowledge; your own point of healing.
www.youhealit.com

Murry Handler: My writing is my escape, my love, my repose. I am primarily a painter, a fine artist whose work is not easy for people to understand. My poetry is more understandable. I write in short lines and it's like singing to myself, clarifying my thoughts. In some ways my poetry is much like painting, changing and adjusting as days pass. It's my way to get the stresses of life out of my system.

Meg Wethington is a poet and spoken word artist residing in New Bern, North Carolina. She enthusiastically serves as the President of The Bohemian Artists of New Bern and on the board of the local non-profit Community Artist Will. www.communityartistwill.org; megwethington@gmail.com

Richard Smyth earned his Ph.D. in English from the University of Florida. He edits the poetry journal Albatross, and his poems have appeared in Tampa Review, Kansas Quarterly, Florida Review, Southern Poetry Review. He currently teaches technology in public school.

Steve Bloom was founder and host of the Activist Poet's Roundtable and the Poetry for Social Activists workshop, both in New York City. Currently he is curator of the "Poetry Corner" for the Southern Anti-Racism Network (SARN http://www.projectsarn.org/). Visit his website at www.stevebloompoetry.net.

The Heron Clan III Acknowledgments:

Stan Absher, **I Close My Accounts:** Published as *"How the VP of Banking Closes His Account" (Bay Leaf Fall 2011)* **The Boar:** *Paulus Silentiarius (Greek Anthology, Book VI, 168)*; **Titmouse:** (JS Absher, *Night Weather,* (Cynosura Press, *2010*).

Asha Gowan, **Fireflies:** http://rasputinpoetry.blogspot.com/2014/11/fireflies-flying-their-fire-fireflies.html.

Robert Okaji, **What Edges Hold:** (*Boston Review*, April 2014); **Ritual:** (*Middle Gray*, October 2013); **With These Nine Fingers:** (*Clade Song*, 3, 2013).

Yeon-seong Park, **Like a Picnic and Chung Yang's Yard:** Copyright© 2001 by Lori Chu and Yeon-seong Park, used by permission of the authors); **Red Fruit** and **Cobweb Castle:** (*Dances With Anticipating Ants,* (Chonnam University Press, 2006); **Dandelion Blues** (*Gwangju News).*

Arnold Johanson, **The Philosopher** and **A Little Behind in His Thinking** appeared in Main Street Rag. **Well Tempered in Leipzig** appeared in Arnie Johanson, *A Man and A Horse* (Ortenstone Press, 2007).

Bruce Lader, **After a Visit from the Angel of Insomnia Relief:** (*Solo Novo,* v. 2,Solo Press 2012); **When Cats Could Fly** (*Cloudbank,* Number 3, 2010) **Our Own Blood** *Landscapes of Longing* by Bruce Lader (Main Street Rag 2009); **Reverse Noir** *Fugitive Hope* by Bruce Lader, (Červená Barva Press 2014).

Doug Stuber, **Pablo and Max:** (*The Road Not Taken, Journal of Formal Poetry*, 2013; **We've Woven a Web**: *Open Secrets, Top Secrets,* Chonnam University Press, 2013); **The Shining Path:** (*The Hazmat Review #1,* January 1996); **Play:** (*The Obelisk,* Spring 1983, St. Petersburg College).

.

Jaki Shelton Green, **a litany for the possessed,** *breath of the song, New and Selected Poems* by Jaki Shelton Green, (Carolina Wren Press); **humble light for Imani**: (*When Women Waken Poetry Anthology*).

Ed Lyons, **Ode to Solitude:** (The Obelisk, Spring 1983, St. Petersburg College); **Dry Season:** (Mangrove Review, 1984-85,University of Florida); **The Wild Rose:** *Poets for Peace,* (Chapel Hill Press, 2002).

Jasmine Farrell, **Better Without You:** (*My Quintessence,* by Jasmine Farrell, 2014).

Meg Wethington, **Visit** and **Jazz** (*Honest Living* by Meg Wethington).

Artists

Cover Art: Ronald Bryant

Ronald Bryant was born in Durham, NC. Creatively sketching as a child in wet clay and sand marked the genesis of his interest in visual arts. An early love of books quickly transformed his playful sketching into intense passion. Early exposure to artistic luminaries such as Michelangelo and Leonardo paved the way for a life-long commitment to study and practice. Although primarily a sculptor, the artist works in acrylics, oils, and a variety of other color mediums when painting.

The ability to draw in black and white is the core skill that he considers indispensable to his art. The underlying philosophy in all his work is that a collective knowledge of sculpture, drawing, and painting informs and enhances whatever single discipline chosen in a richer and fuller way. Most of his work hangs in private collections in the area.

Commissions from movie producers, fine art portraiture, to commercial illustration assignments are included in his collected works. Largely self-taught, the artist received formal training from the Art Institute of Pittsburg, Pennsylvania and the Art Institute of Raleigh, Durham, North Carolina. The struggle for human rights has been a life-long interest and is the central focus of his latest work.

Note the diversity of the front and back covers, both by Ron.

Interior Ink on Paper: Murry Handler

Born in Bangor, Me., Murry Handler moved to NYC as a young man, just out of the navy, to study art and seek a career in the advertising/graphic design field. His art training included 3 years at The Franklin Institute of Art, figure drawing with Joseph Kelly at Pratt Institute and painting at the Workshop School under the late, great Joe Hirsh. He then went on to a professional career as an illustrator, graphic designer, adjunct instructor at The Fashion Institute of Technology and Parsons School of Design, and owner of a 14 person advertising/design studio.

His work in advertising/design won numerous awards and is cited in many volumes of the Creativity Annual published by Art Direction Book Co.

In addition to his creative work as an artist, Murry is a gifted poet with two books of poetry, illustrated with his original drawings in handmade and hand-bound covers. His memoir, Almost A Jew, has a cover illustrated with a repro of his limited edition print 'Dejection' which is most unlike his usual state of joyous optimism. Murry is at work now on a second book "From My Side of the Hill". When not otherwise occupied Murry prunes, wires and cares for his amazing collection of 50 year old bonsai trees.

He's a member of the Society of Illustrators, NYC and is represented by FrAnk Gallery in Chapel Hill, NC.

"No matter how many paintings I have completed, every painting is still an experiment to me. I don't want to know how my painting will end, I want the surprise of finding the end, sometimes quite by accident."

Murry's art can be found on pages 22, 39, 67, 84, 104, 117 and 148.

Support wildlife: attend a poetry reading some time soon.